Dealing with Bullies

ORMSKIRK
LEARNER ZONE

ISSUES

Volume 73

D1103589

Editor

Craig Donnellan

 *Independence*

Educational Publishers
Cambridge

First published by Independence
PO Box 295
Cambridge CB1 3XP
England

British Library Cataloguing in Publication Data
Dealing with Bullies – (Issues Series)
I. Donnellan, Craig II. Series
302.3'4

ISBN 1 86168 255 7

Printed in Great Britain
MWL Print Group Ltd

Typeset by
Claire Boyd

Cover
The illustration on the front cover is by
Pumpkin House.

CONTENTS

Chapter One: Bullying at School

Chapter Two: Workplace Bullying

Introduction

Dealing with Bullies is the seventy-third volume in the **Issues** series. The aim of this series is to offer up-to-date information about important issues in our world.

Dealing with Bullies looks at the issues of bullying in the school and in the workplace.

The information comes from a wide variety of sources and includes:
Government reports and statistics
Newspaper reports and features
Magazine articles and surveys
Web site material
Literature from lobby groups
and charitable organisations.

It is hoped that, as you read about the many aspects of the issues explored in this book, you will critically evaluate the information presented. It is important that you decide whether you are being presented with facts or opinions. Does the writer give a biased or an unbiased report? If an opinion is being expressed, do you agree with the writer?

Dealing with Bullies offers a useful starting-point for those who need convenient access to information about the many issues involved. However, it is only a starting-point. At the back of the book is a list of organisations which you may want to contact for further information.

*****

Half the population are bullied . . . ◆ ◆ ◆

. . . most only recognise it when they read this

Read through the following checklists and learn how to recognise the bullies in your life and the harm they cause to you and others.

Where are people bullied?

- at work by their manager or co-workers or subordinates, or by their clients (bullying, workplace bullying, mobbing, work abuse, harassment, discrimination)
- at home by their partner or parents or siblings or children (bullying, assault, domestic violence, abuse, verbal abuse)
- at school (bullying, harassment, assault)
- in the care of others, such as in hospital, convalescent homes, care homes, residential homes (bullying, harassment, assault)
- in the armed forces (bullying, harassment, discrimination, assault)
- by those in authority (harassment, abuse of power)
- by neighbours and landlords (bullying, harassment)
- by strangers (harassment, stalking, assault, sexual assault, rape, grievous bodily harm, murder)

How do you know if you're being bullied?

Bullying differs from harassment and assault in that the latter can result from a single incident or small number of incidents – which everybody recognises as harassment or assault – whereas bullying tends to be an accumulation of many small incidents over a long period of time. Each incident tends to be trivial, and on its own and out of context does not constitute an offence or grounds for disciplinary or grievance action. So . . .

What is bullying?

- constant nit-picking, fault-finding and criticism of a trivial nature – the triviality, regularity and frequency betray bullying; often there is a grain of truth (but only a grain) in the criticism to fool you into believing the criticism has validity, which it does not; often, the criticism is based on distortion, mis-representation or fabrication
- simultaneous with the criticism, a constant refusal to acknowledge you and your contributions and achievements or to recognise your existence and value
- constant attempts to undermine you and your position, status, worth, value and potential

- where you are in a group (e.g. at work), being singled out and treated differently; for instance, everyone else can get away with murder but the moment you put a foot wrong – however trivial – action is taken against you
- being isolated and separated from colleagues, excluded from what's going on, marginalised, overruled, ignored, sidelined, frozen out, sent to Coventry
- being belittled, demeaned and patronised, especially in front of others
- being humiliated, shouted at and threatened, often in front of others
- being overloaded with work, or having all your work taken away and replaced with either menial tasks (filing, photocopying, minute taking) or with no work at all
- finding that your work – and the credit for it – is stolen and plagiarised
- having your responsibility increased but your authority taken away
- having annual leave, sickness leave, and – especially – compassionate leave refused
- being denied training necessary for you to fulfil your duties
- having unrealistic goals set, which change as you approach them
- ditto deadlines which are changed at short notice – or no notice – and without you being informed until it's too late
- finding that everything you say and do is twisted, distorted and misrepresented
- being subjected to disciplinary procedures with verbal or written warnings imposed for trivial or

fabricated reasons and without proper investigation

■ being coerced into leaving through no fault of your own, constructive dismissal, early or ill-health retirement, etc.

How do I recognise a bully?

Most bullying is traceable to one person, male or female – bullying is not a gender issue. Bullies are often clever people (especially female bullies) but you can be clever too.

Who does this describe in your life?

■ Jekyll & Hyde nature – vicious and vindictive in private, but innocent and charming in front of witnesses; no one can (or wants to) believe this individual has a vindictive nature – only the current target sees both sides

■ is a convincing, compulsive liar and when called to account, will make up anything spontaneously to fit their needs at that moment

■ uses lots of charm and is always plausible and convincing when peers, superiors or others are present; the motive of the charm is deception and its purpose is to compensate for lack of empathy

■ relies on mimicry to convince others that they are a 'normal' human being but their words, writing and deeds are hollow, superficial and glib

■ displays a great deal of certitude and self-assuredness to mask their insecurity

■ excels at deception

■ exhibits unusual inappropriate attitudes to sexual matters or sexual behaviour; underneath the charming exterior there are often suspicions or intimations of sexual harassment, sex discrimination or sexual abuse (sometimes racial prejudice as well)

■ exhibits much controlling behaviour and is a control freak

■ displays a compulsive need to criticise whilst simultaneously refusing to acknowledge, value and praise others

■ when called upon to share or address the needs and concerns of others, responds with impatience, irritability and aggression

■ often has an overwhelming, unhealthy and narcissistic need to portray themselves as a wonderful, kind, caring and compassionate person, in contrast to their behaviour and treatment of others; the bully is oblivious to the discrepancy between how they like to be seen (and believe they are seen), and how they are actually seen

■ has an overbearing belief in their qualities of leadership but cannot distinguish between leadership (maturity, decisiveness, assertiveness, trust and integrity) and bullying (immaturity, impulsiveness, aggression, distrust and deceitfulness)

■ when called to account, immediately and aggressively denies everything, then counter-attacks with distorted or fabricated criticisms and allegations; if this is insufficient, quickly feigns victimhood, often by bursting into tears (the purpose is to avoid answering the question and thus evade accountability by manipulating others through the use of guilt)

■ is also . . . aggressive, devious, manipulative, spiteful, vengeful, doesn't listen, can't sustain mature adult conversation, lacks a conscience, shows no remorse, is drawn to power, emotionally cold and flat, humourless, joyless, ungrateful, dysfunctional, disruptive, divisive, rigid and inflexible, selfish, insincere, insecure, immature and deeply inadequate, especially in interpersonal skills

I estimate one person in thirty has this behaviour profile. I describe them as having a disordered personality: an aggressive but intelligent individual who expresses their

---

Most bullying is traceable to one person, male or female – bullying is not a gender issue. Bullies are often clever people but you can be clever too

---

violence psychologically (constant criticism etc.) rather than physically (assault).

What does bullying do to my health?

Bullying causes injury to health and makes you ill. How many of these symptoms do you have?

■ constant high levels of stress and anxiety

■ frequent illness such as viral infections especially flu and glandular fever, colds, coughs, chest, ear, nose and throat infections (stress plays havoc with your immune system)

■ aches and pains in the joints and muscles with no obvious cause; also back pain with no obvious cause and which won't go away or respond to treatment

■ headaches and migraines

■ tiredness, exhaustion, constant fatigue

■ sleeplessness, nightmares, waking early, waking up more tired than when you went to bed

■ flashbacks and replays, obsessiveness, can't get the bullying out of your mind

■ irritable bowel syndrome

■ skin problems such as eczema, psoriasis, athlete's foot, ulcers, shingles, urticaria

■ poor concentration, can't concentrate on anything for long

■ bad or intermittently-functioning memory, forgetfulness, especially with trivial day-to-day things

■ sweating, trembling, shaking, palpitations, panic attacks

■ tearfulness, bursting into tears regularly and over trivial things

■ uncharacteristic irritability and angry outbursts

■ hypervigilance (feels like but is not paranoia), being constantly on edge

■ hypersensitivity, fragility, isolation, withdrawal

■ reactive depression, a feeling of woebegoneness, lethargy, hopelessness, anger, futility and more

■ shattered self-confidence, low self-worth, low self-esteem, loss of self-love, etc.

■ The above information is from Success Unlimited's web site which can be found at www.bullyonline.org

© *Success Unlimited*

On-line bullying

1 in 4 children are the victims of 'on-line bullying'

1 in 4 children in the UK have been bullied or threatened via their mobile phone or PC according to a survey commissioned by leading UK children's charity NCH. The results, announced today (15 April 2003), have led NCH to call for greater awareness of the problem amongst parents and teachers, and better education for children and young people on how to deal with 21st-century bullying techniques.

Mobile phones appear to be the most commonly abused medium with 16% of young people saying they'd received bullying or threatening text messages, followed by 7% who had been harassed in Internet chat-rooms and 4% via e-mail. Worryingly when asked who they had reported the bullying to, 29% of those surveyed said that they told no one. Of the 69% who did tell someone 42% turned to a friend and 32% to a parent.

John Carr, Associate Director of NCH's Children and Technology Unit, says: 'On-line bullying is a modern menace which needs to be addressed. If we want our children to benefit from all the good things IT has to offer, we need to protect them from the risks it poses.

'NCH's concern is that children as young as 11 are being faced with taunts or threats from an often anonymous source. They're either not telling anyone and suffering in silence, or are confiding in people who themselves don't know how to deal with it effectively. The more people know that it happens, the easier it will be for children to cope with on-line bullying.'

NCH has three simple pieces of advice for children and young people to remember:
- Don't put up with bullying! Always tell someone you trust what's happening – your Mum or Dad, a teacher or a friend – and try to find a way to stop it.
- Always be careful who you give your mobile phone number or e-mail address out to. If you do start being bullied through your phone or computer, your mobile phone or Internet service provider can help you by changing your number or address.
- If you receive messages that upset or frighten you, make a record of the times and dates you received them, and report them to the police.

Mobile phones appear to be the most commonly abused medium with 16% of young people saying they'd received bullying or threatening text messages

---

NCH believes that this issue is the responsibility of everyone – parents, the education system and the industry. It recommends that:

- all schools should amend their bullying policies to include text and on-line abuse and make a commitment to educate teachers, as well as pupils;
- all parents should make sure they know who to contact and what to do if their child is a victim and talk the issue through with their family ;
- all ISPs and mobile phone companies should take responsibility for finding effective ways of dealing with complaints and providing advice on the subject to their users.

Parents, teachers and children can find further details on how to deal with Internet safety issues on the NCH IT OK web site – www.nch.org.uk/itok

NCH also run bullying workshops in schools across the UK. To find out more you can e-mail bullyhelp@nch.org.uk

■ The above information is from NCH's web site which can be found at www.nch.org.uk

© NCH

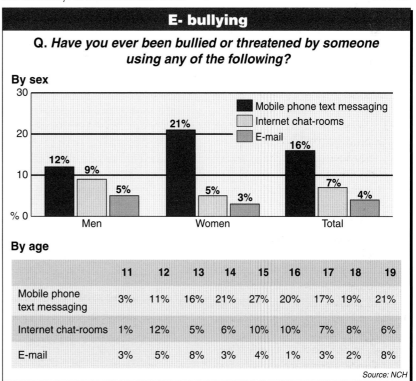

E- bullying

Q. Have you ever been bullied or threatened by someone using any of the following?

By sex

Legend: Mobile phone text messaging / Internet chat-rooms / E-mail

Men: 12%, 9%, 5%
Women: 21%, 5%, 3%
Total: 16%, 7%, 4%

By age

	11	12	13	14	15	16	17	18	19
Mobile phone text messaging	3%	11%	16%	21%	27%	20%	17%	19%	21%
Internet chat-rooms	1%	12%	5%	6%	10%	10%	7%	8%	6%
E-mail	3%	5%	8%	3%	4%	1%	3%	2%	8%

Source: NCH

Bullying by mobile phone and cell phone

Abusive text messages and bullying by text messaging

Mobile phones have become the new weapon of choice for bullies. With three-quarters of children now owning a mobile phone, the anonymity, the sluggishness of telecommunications service providers, and the weakness of law provide bullies with the perfect means of taunting their target with little fear of being caught. Text messages provide complete anonymity.

Many pay-as-you-go mobile phones can be bought over the counter and do not require proof of identity, nor is any record kept of the new owner. Calls made from these types of mobile phone are virtually untraceable.

What can you do?

Never ignore threats, either verbal or by phone or via text message. But don't respond in the way the bully wants you to. When people advise you to 'just ignore it', what they really mean is 'do not respond to the taunts and provocation or engage the bullies, but take careful note of what is being done to you, who is doing it and how, and log all of this in a diary, then immediately get your parents involved and develop a strategy for dealing with it which you are all agreed on'. So read on . . .

Understand what bullying is so that when it starts you can stay in control and nip it in the bud. Do your homework now.

Do not underestimate the distress and the destructive effect that constant bullying and harassment can have on the recipient and their family.

Get help immediately from a trusted parent – you cannot handle bullying alone. Adults cannot handle bullying by themselves. The bullies, who operate outside social norms, will try to isolate and separate you from friends, family and parents, but don't be fooled.

Learn to recognise the early signs and keep a detailed diary. Print off the messages if you are able, otherwise make a careful note of every one, the date, time, the caller-ID if available, or the reason for the caller-ID being unavailable (e.g. 'withheld', 'unavailable', etc.) – even this can prove useful.

Bullies derive gratification – a perverse sense of satisfaction – from the power and control they exert over their victim. The aim of bullies is power, control, domination and subjugation. Bullies confirm the power and control by use of provocation. When the target responds, it's a sign that the bully has successfully exerted control. They jerk your string, you jump. By refusing to jump, you deny the bully their sense of satisfaction.

Never ignore threats, either verbal or by phone or via text message. But don't respond in the way the bully wants you to

---

Stay in control. This is a game – a nasty game, but a game. Learn the rules of the game: it's about power and control. Tell yourself repeatedly that the threats, accusations, allegations, criticisms etc. have nothing whatsoever to do with you – they are a device for taunting, a fabrication, a deception, but most of all, a projection of the bully's own weaknesses, shortcomings, and failings. Every nasty word is an admission by the bully about themselves.

Sometimes the accusations, allegations, criticisms and taunts contain within them a grain of truth. This grain of truth is there to fool you into thinking that all the abuse is true, which it isn't. Don't be fooled by this trick.

Become a detective. You can work out who is calling and pursue a course of action which will call them to account. It's unlikely you will have the resources to do this by yourself, so get help.

It's almost certain that you know the person who is sending you abusive text messages or calls. Think through your list of 'friends' and family and ask yourself who might be doing this. You might be surprised at how close this person is or how well you know them. The most common triggers for bullying are rejection, jealousy and envy – who might this apply to?

If the bullying gets out of control, consider getting a second mobile phone and giving the number only to close family. Give the number to only one person at a time and keep a careful log of who you've given it to and when. Oblige everyone to whom you've given it not to give the number to anyone else. Do this in collaboration with a trusted parent and don't tell anyone else that you are keeping a diary. Regard your old mobile phone as a source of evidence. Every abusive call is more evidence. If the calls reach such a level that you need to involve the police, perhaps they might want to look after your old mobile phone. Then there's a peculiar delight in knowing that every time the bully makes abusive calls or posts offensive text messages these are going straight to the police station.

In the UK the law is weak but you may be able to use the Protection From Harassment Act, which has both civil and criminal provisions. Bullying, especially by mobile phone, is very similar to stalking.

■ The above information is from Success Unlimited's web site which can be found at www.bullyonline.org

© *Success Unlimited*

If looks could kill

Young women and bullying

Bullying is widespread. In a recent large-scale survey in Britain, more than half the young people questioned had been bullied and one in ten had been severely bullied. A third of the girls and a quarter of the boys had at some time been afraid of going to school because of bullying (Katz et al 2001). Over 20,000 calls were made to ChildLine about bullying last year and it was the single most cited issue by callers (Twigg 2002).

What is bullying?

There are many definitions of bullying. The following is from Olweus (1991), a leading researcher on bullying. His definition is: 'When a young person is exposed repeatedly and over time to intentional, negative, aggressive behaviour from an individual or group. This can be physical, verbal, spreading rumours or by excluding someone. Bullying involves an imbalance of power. It is also bullying when a young person is teased repeatedly. But it is not bullying when two young people of the same strength have the odd fight or quarrel.'

Young people themselves have described bullying as:
'*Jealousy . . . emotional and physical abuse . . . racism . . . nasty teasing . . . mouthing off . . . bitchiness . . . ganging up on people . . . hitting . . . leaving people out . . . saying they are gay . . . rape . . . force . . . nicking people's money . . . taking the mick . . . dodgy looks . . . road rage . . . criticising . . . threatening . . . piss-taking . . . prejudice . . . no respect . . . being mean and abusing a person's pride*' (TSA 2002).

Bullying can include all kinds of negative behaviour, both direct and indirect, which is designed to hurt and humiliate. The main defining feature of this behaviour is that it involves a systematic abuse of power – there is a perpetrator who exerts power and control and a victim who is helpless and powerless.

Young women's experiences of bullying

In a recent study of 3,000 girls, over half had been bullied and 12 per cent had been severely bullied (Katz et al 2001). It has been suggested that girls are more involved in sustained bullying than boys (Ofsted 2001) and that it is girls who report more fear of attending school because of bullying (Schools Health Education Unit 2000). Girls themselves highlighted bullying as a major issue for them personally, or for their fellow students, in a recent study of girls' school experiences (Osler et al 2002). The bullying can take a number of forms:

Sexual bullying / harassment

Sexual bullying is characterised by abusive name calling; looks and comments about appearance, attractiveness or emerging puberty; inappropriate and uninvited touching; sexual innuendoes and propositions; pornographic material; graffiti with sexual content. In its most extreme form, sexual bullying may lead to sexual assault or rape (Smith 2002). Young women bear the brunt of sexual bullying and harassment. In a recent study, four out of five young women reported having experienced at least one kind of harassment (Regan and Kelly 2001). Research in the early nineties suggested that boys were responsible for a large part of the bullying that girls are subjected to (Olweus 1991).

Girl-to-girl cruelty

Early research into bullying tended to focus on boy aggressors and their direct, physically aggressive behaviours. However, more recent studies have indicated that girls, too, can bully, but they use different methods (for example Leckie 1998). While boys are more likely to use direct methods such as physical attack or verbal abuse, girls tend to use more covert, indirect methods such as spreading rumours, writing nasty notes and excluding and ostracising others. Girls have also become very adept at using new technologies such as text messaging to inflict mental pain.

The tighter social structures of which girls are a part, make it easier for them to exploit relationships and manipulate and harm other girls in these indirect ways. This type of bullying can be particularly devastating and also difficult to detect and stop. As one girl put it:

'If a boy's going to bully he'll use violence. Girls do it mentally because they're clever. They know it hurts more' (Michelle/Osler et al 2002).

The assertion that 'it hurts more' has been backed up by research which found that non-physical ways of being bullied were more consistently related to emotional distress than physical ways of being bullied (Hawker 1998).

Racist bullying

In racist bullying, a young person is targeted for representing a group and attacking the individual sends a message to that group. Racist bullying not only hurts the victim, but also other young people from the same group and their families. Incidents

most commonly include verbal abuse by name calling, racist jokes and offensive mimicry; physical threats or attacks and racist graffiti (Smith 2002).

Recent studies of girls' experiences of bullying have indicated that race and country of origin are frequently a focus of bullying. In one study, nearly a quarter of girls who had been severely bullied had experienced racism (Katz et al 2001).

In another study both white and minority ethnic students reported observing or experiencing bullying based on ethnicity or country of origin:

'I don't think there should be racism in school. There is a lot of that in school . . . racism. I was bullied when I was in Year Seven. "You eat curries" . . . a lot of that . . . "you shouldn't be here, this isn't your country" and things like that . . . and I didn't really like that' (Usha/Osler et al 2002).

Homophobic bullying

Young lesbians or those perceived to be lesbian are particularly vulnerable to abuse and harassment. A large-scale study by Stonewall found that 79 per cent of young people who were lesbian or gay had been called names and 44 per cent had been harassed by fellow students because of their sexuality (Mason and Palmer 1996). Another study found that 51 per cent of schools reported at least one incident of homophobic bullying occurring in the last term, but only six per cent of schools had bullying policies that specifically mentioned homophobic bullying (Douglas et al 1997).

The existence of Section 28 means that teachers are often reluctant to discuss homosexuality and homophobia. As one young lesbian described her teacher's reluctance: 'She refuses to discuss "gay" topics in class' (Mason and Palmer 1996). This leads to a climate of ignorance, fear and abuse, that teachers are either unaware of or feel powerless to deal with.

Effects of being bullied

Bullying can have serious negative consequences on young women's health and wellbeing and on their future opportunities in life.

> *While boys are more likely to use direct methods such as physical attack or verbal abuse, girls tend to use more covert, indirect methods*

Health consequences

Victims of bullying may suffer from a variety of physical complaints such as fits, faints, vomiting, limb pains, paralysis, hyperventilation, visual symptoms, headaches, stomach aches, bed wetting, sleeping difficulties and sadness (Smith 2002). In addition to physical problems, being bullied has serious consequences for mental health.

Young people who are bullied are more likely to show signs of general depression, suicidal thoughts and somatic complaints than those who are not (Rigby and Slee 1993).

Compared to those girls who were not bullied, severely bullied girls are twice as likely to say that they hardly ever feel happy and confident about themselves (Katz et al 2001). Most shocking is the finding that more than one in four girls who had experienced violence from bullies had made a suicide attempt (Katz et al 2001). It is estimated that in the UK, at least 16 children commit suicide each year because of bullying and a new term: 'bullycide' has been coined to describe this tragic phenomenon (Marr and Field 2001).

The effects of bullying can continue long into adult life. In a recent study in which adults were questioned about their experiences of being bullied as children, respondents were found to have low self-esteem, suicidal thoughts and difficulty relating to people (Kidscape 1999).

These problems may be particularly acute for young women who have experienced the psychological-style bullying typical of girl aggressors. Being excluded from their friendship group can completely undermine their confidence and self-esteem. Their feelings of inadequacy are turned inwards and may manifest themselves in a range of self-harming behaviours such as self-injury, drug and alcohol abuse, eating disorders and abusive relationships. Recent research found that almost three times more severely bullied girls had tried drugs as a release from depression or tension than other girls (Katz et al 2001).

Educational achievement

Bullying not only causes severe distress, it also affects how young people perform in school. Victims may be very reluctant to attend school and are often absent. In research carried out by the Department for Education and Skills, a third of all girls said they had been too afraid to go to school at some point in their lives.

One of the main coping mechanisms for girls experiencing bullying is to exclude themselves from school. A recent study has indicated that this withdrawal tends to go largely undetected because of the greater focus placed on managing the more overt challenges to school authority posed by boys (Osler et al 2002). Girls appear to 'get away with' their absenteeism, as they find ways of disguising it such as forging sick notes, signing in at registration and then skipping lessons and faking illnesses, including the effects of menstruation. Osler's study found that many girls who truant actually want to be in education, but truant as a way of avoiding difficulties such as bullying:

'I've got two friends who don't come to school sometimes 'cause they get bullied and they just go home. They don't really stay home because they want to . . . it's because of the bullying' (Usha/Osler 2002).

The more frequent the absences, the harder it gets to catch up with school work and girls find themselves in a downward spiral that may end up with them dropping out altogether. Career options are then very limited. Lack of qualifications coupled with low self-worth may result in early motherhood, which in turn may lead to poverty and social exclusion.

Responses to bullying

The Government's approach

Since September 1999 there has been a specific duty placed on head

teachers under the Schools Standards and Framework Act to develop policies to prevent all forms of bullying. Policies must comply with the Human Rights Act 1998 and the Race Amendment Act 2000. The latter requires schools to draw up a race equality policy and ensure policies do not discriminate against racial groups.

The Department for Education and Skills has just updated its anti-bullying pack for schools. 'Don't Suffer in Silence' gives ideas about how to draw up an anti-bullying policy and suggests a range of ways of tackling bullying and involving parents. It includes examples of approaches that have proved helpful, such as circle time, befriending, mentoring, mediation and active listening. Advice and information for pupils, teachers and parents is also available on the department's website: www.dfes.gov.uk/bullying

Schools' approach

Although all schools are required by law to have an anti-bullying policy, this in itself doesn't guarantee that bullying is being addressed. In a recent survey, three-quarters of the young people questioned felt that their school does not have an effective anti-bullying policy that works (Katz 2001).

There are a variety of reasons why schools may not be tackling bullying effectively. Policies may be out of date, weak, not publicised, good on paper but not upheld or applied inconsistently. Often there

is no regular monitoring and evaluation of approaches taken. There may be resistance from staff to recognise there is a problem; a lack of confidentiality which means that pupils are unwilling to speak out, or no effective consequences for bullies – so they are seen to get away with it. Even when there has been a lot of dedicated work on bullying, the effect may fade with time or as staff change.

For young women there is the added difficulty that bullying amongst girls is not easily recognised or perceived as a problem. It is easier for teachers to identify and address the more physical forms of bullying than the subtle, psychological bullying that is more typically engaged in by girls. While girls themselves have highlighted bullying as a serious issue facing them in school, professionals interviewed in a recent study tended to give it a lower priority, only partially recognising the detrimental effects of psychological bullying on girls' concentration and learning (Osler 2002). The tendency to internalise their responses to problems such as bullying means that girls' needs often go unnoticed. Faced with a range of competing pressures, teachers are likely to focus on the more overt needs of boys and the more immediate challenges they present in the classroom.

■ The above information is from the YWCA. Visit their web site at www.ywca-gb.org.uk

© YWCA

Bullying, what to do, what not to do

Unfortunately bullying is very common in schools and in places of work everywhere. Most people think of bullying as physical – hitting, punching, kicking, and stealing; but bullying is anything that makes a person do something they do not want to do, name calling etc. The main problem is that too many people and too many schools stand by and let it happen.

You as a pupil have certain rights, your school must do certain things to protect you from bullying. The following information came from the DFES (Department for Education and Skills) – these guys are responsible for writing the laws that tell teachers and schools how to work. Their website is at http://www.dfes.gov.uk

'Each school should have a clear school behaviour policy. It should make clear the boundaries of what is acceptable, the hierarchy of sanctions, arrangements for their consistent and fair application, and a linked system of rewards for good behaviour.

'It should promote respect for others, intolerance of bullying and harassment, the importance of self-discipline and the difference between "right" and "wrong".'

Unfortunately we cannot guarantee you will never be bullied.

There are some things that you can do, however, that will make you less likely to be bullied:

What to do

- Remember: You don't deserve to be bullied, it's the bullies' problem!
- Talk about it to someone who will listen
- Ignore the bullies themselves completely:

'The best thing to bullies about bullying people is seeing that they are hurting the victim. That's what gives them the kick. Simply learn to ignore them. If you shut them out and carry on, they will eventually get bored of not getting a response, and leave you alone. It's a tried and tested method – proved by my experience! Try it, it really works.'

Posted by Jonathon –
26/02/00 7:45 pm

- Tell a teacher you trust
- Stick to facts and bring a witness
- Defend yourself only if necessary
- Stay in a group
- Be firm, if they pressure you shout 'NO'; it'll get attention

What not to do

- Do not ignore the bullying – make a noise about it
- Don't confront the bully
- Don't fight back except to defend yourself – it only makes it worse believe me!
- Don't get in a slanging match
- If you are scared or intimidated get away and get help
- Don't fight to keep your stuff – you are more important!

Other advice

- Stand up for yourself – do not become a doormat – if someone teases you do not stand for it; tell your teacher, friends or anyone. It does help.
- Speak to other people who have been bullied, they will know what to do.
- If your teachers do not listen or take action make a row – you have a right.
- Don't let anyone fob you off with the idea that your problems are not as significant as anyone else's! Cos they are far from it – everyone counts! Do not be afraid to show your individuality. If people around you at the moment don't like it, people around the corner will!
- Bullies (although it doesn't seem like it) are only confident from the outside. I personally don't buy that crap about them already being scarred and having to take it out on others – They are cowards!

■ The above information is from Pupiline's web site which can be found at www.pupiline.net

©2003 Pupiline Limited

Fear of being bullied

Do you ever feel afraid of going to school because of bullying?

	Never	Sometimes	Often	Very Often
Year 6 Males	71%	24%	3%	3%
Year 6 Females	58%	35%	4%	3%
Year 8 Males	72%	21%	3%	3%
Year 8 Females	63%	27%	5%	5%
Year 10 Males	82%	14%	2%	2%
Year 10 Females	74%	20%	3%	2%

Valid responses

Year 6 Males (10-11 years)	6,443
Year 6 Females	6,343
Year 8 Males (12-13 years)	6,481
Year 8 Females	7,089
Year 10 Males (14-15 years)	6,627
Year 10 Females	7,128

1. 18-42% of the year/gender groups fear bullying at least sometimes.

2. The females are more fearful than the males, and the Year 6s are more concerned than the Year 10s.

Source: Schools Health Education Unit (SHEU)

'I sometimes bully people. What can I do?'

Information from Kidscape

Most people have bullied someone at some point in their lives but they usually feel sorry about it afterwards and try not to do it again. However, if you are constantly picking on other people and you don't care how angry or upset you make them, then you've got a problem.

Admitting that you sometimes bully other people can be hard but we all have to face up to what we do and how we make others feel. No one really likes bullies. If you want to be liked for yourself then you should try and change the way you treat other people. Bullies might frighten people into being nice to them but this isn't friendship – bullies are usually lonely and unhappy.

> 'We thought one girl in our year was fat – she probably wasn't really, but we went on and on at her about it. She suddenly started to lose weight, and then we found out that she had become anorexic. In the end, she had to go into hospital. I feel ashamed about it now.'
>
> Vicky, 18

If you are a bully, then you can change – even if you like yourself as a bully!

First of all, try and work out why you bully others.

- do you mean to upset or hurt others? When you talk to people do you want them to feel small and intimidated?
- do you know when you are bullying or is it people's reactions which tell you that you have done something wrong?
- is something making you miserable? A problem at home or at school?
- do you feel left out or lonely at school?
- is someone picking on you? A teacher, another adult, someone in your family, another pupil?

How does this make you feel? Do you take your bad feeling out on someone else? Could you try to talk to this person to see if you can sort out the problem yourself? Could someone else talk to them for you?

- is there a particular person that you pick on? Why do you target him or her? Are you jealous of them? If there is someone who really bugs you, try and stay out of their way.

If you are a bully, then you can change – even if you like yourself as a bully!

- do particular occasions irritate you so that you take out your feelings on others? Can you pinpoint exactly what annoys you the most – could you change whatever it is? Think of ways to avoid these situations or make up your mind that if you do get

ARE YOU OKAY?

...YOU HAVEN'T BULLIED US TODAY...

...I AM OKAY!

caught up in them again, you'll walk away before you do anything you might regret.

- does something (a particular lesson or task) make you feel angry or frustrated? Do you find some subjects really hard? Can you talk to someone about the problem?
- do you feel that you are letting someone down by not being clever enough or talented enough, or polite enough? Sometimes families or teachers can set such high standards of achievement that we feel we can never match up to what they expect of us. This can be totally demoralising. Often these people don't realise that they are laying such a burden on us. If you feel like this talk to them about it and explain how you feel.

'I suppose I just messed around most of the time at school. I had a couple of mates and we used to make the younger kids pay us every week or we'd give them a right knocking. We must have been pretty frightening. None of that's much good to me now.'

Darren, 17

- do you go around with a gang which bullies people? Why do you stay with the gang? Do you really want to be with people who are always picking on others?
- do you get a thrill from hurting other people or taking their things? Does this make you feel powerful?
- are you bigger and stronger than other people your age? Do you use your size and strength to intimidate others?
- do you identify with violence and cruelty? Why? Were or are you the victim of violence? If so, you can break the cycle of violence and make sure no one has to suffer like you did.

Is there someone you trust that you could talk to about the problem?

'I didn't know how bad victims felt until my brother was bullied. He's 3 years younger than me and he has to wear a hearing aid. The bullying he went through made him into a wreck until we got it stopped. I realised I'd made kids feel like that. I wouldn't bully anyone now.'

Rob, 15

Discussing things with someone else often helps to make things clearer. It can be hard to change ingrained habits and having someone else on your side will make things easier.

- The above information is an extract from *You can beat bullying – A guide for young people* which is produced by Kidscape. Copies of this publication, in colour and with graphics, can be ordered from Kidscape. See page 41 for their address details.

© Kidscape

Stress of young bullying victims

Young victims of bullying can suffer from clinically significant levels of post-traumatic stress, new research has revealed.

And verbal abuse can have more impact upon victims' self-worth than physical attacks such as punching, doctors warned.

Psychologist Dr Stephen Joseph studied 331 school pupils in England and found as many as 40% had been bullied at some point during their education.

He devised a 'victim scale' to assess the effects of different types of bullying.

It covered physical victimisation, verbal taunts, social mani-pulation and attacks on property such as the theft or destruction of belongings.

Dr Joseph, of the University of Warwick, found bullying of all types lowered youngsters' self-esteem.

Social manipulation, such as excluding the victim from taking part in games, was more likely to lead to post-traumatic stress

---

But social manipulation, such as excluding the victim from taking part in games, was more likely to lead to post-traumatic stress.

He also found verbal taunts in particular resulted in lower self-worth.

'This study reveals that bullying and particularly name calling can be degrading for adolescents,' he said.

'It is important that peer victimisation is taken seriously as symptoms such as insomnia, anxiety and depression are common among victims and have a negative impact on psychological health.'

© *The Daily Mail, April 2003*

Hidden damage

Schools are being encouraged to take steps to stamp out homophobic bullying. Polly Curtis reports

Tackling bullying is on the agenda of every school. But there are areas in which it can get missed. 'Homophobia is not dealt with effectively in schools at all. It is still a massive taboo in education. It is made worse by misconception about Section 28,' says Becky, a teacher from north London.

But yesterday new guidelines were issued to schools in the north-east as part of a pilot aimed at helping teachers tackle the problem of homophobic bullying in the classroom.

Research shows that up to 40% of young lesbian, gay or bisexual people have attempted suicide because of bullying at school. Three-quarters of those being bullied have a history of truancy.

The guide, *Stamp Out Homophobia*, calls on schools to incorporate anti-homophobic bullying messages into their general anti-bullying policies, or even create a new policy on the subject, confidently communicated to staff, pupils, governors and parents.

It also asks teachers to challenge homophobic language, even when not directed at an individual, to ensure the school is committed to creating a more accepting environment. Such issues, it continues, should be built into the curriculum, particularly in PHSE and citizenship classes.

Howard Ford, youth worker at MesMac, an organisation that provides support for young lesbian, gay and bisexual people in the north-east which helped compile the guidelines, said: 'Schooling can be very negative. Sex and relationship education currently done in schools sometimes ignores the needs of this group of young people. This pack helps schools develop an ethos that every young person has a right to respect and to feel valued and included – no matter what their sexual orientation.'

A spokeswoman from the West End Women and Girl's Centre, in Newcastle, welcomed the guidance, and said: 'It is extremely important for schools to address homophobic bullying, as negative experiences of schools can have a profound impact on the mental and sexual health of young lesbian, gay and bisexual people. It also affects their potential academically and socially.'

> **Research shows that up to 40% of young lesbian, gay or bisexual people have attempted suicide because of bullying at school**

However, as Becky points out, teachers have shied away from positively addressing the issue because of confusion over Section 28, the law designed to prevent homosexuality being promoted in schools. Although the law is not actively enforced in schools it is still law and there are now calls for it to be abolished.

The Department for Education and Skills is clear that schools should take steps to prevent homophobic bullying. Ignoring it could, the department claims, amount to discrimination that could be challenged under the Human Rights Act.

The guidance follows research conducted by MesMac with academics at the College of York St John and Teesside University.

Concentrating on the experiences of young people in schools in the north-east, they found that while 20% of the 15 14- to 26-year-olds interviewed had never been bullied because of their sexual orientation, 75% had been physically assaulted at least once. Two had received death threats.

The report found that in the vast majority of cases the school had failed to provide any support for the victims. In one case, when help was sought by a pupil, the teacher told his parents, without his consent.

The researchers found that 17% of their sample group had attempted suicide and 33% suffered depression when they were being bullied.

Despite the small size of the sample group, researchers say the experiences of young people in their study reflect those of large-scale studies. Particularly on the nature of the bullying.

'Young men will label other young men as "queer" or "gay" if they do not conform to rigid and stereotypical gender roles. Young men who perform well academically, who socialise with young women or who are poor at sports are often labelled "gay",' the report concluded.

Bullying tactics

Saba Salman on a grassroots group which is helping people with learning disabilities cope with verbal abuse

Hilary Cooke, who has a learning disability, was about to step on to a bus when the driver said: 'I don't want you on this bus – you make me feel sick.' Recalling the incident, she says: 'He shut the door right in my face and drove off. I felt numb. Other times, children in the street have called me names, like "spastic" or "fatty". I do try not to take notice but it's hard, very hard.'

She is a member of East Herts People First, a self-help support group based at Hertfordshire Regional College which is behind an innovative project to protect adults with learning disabilities from verbal abuse and harassment.

The campaign was much needed – the region has the highest concentration of people with learning disabilities in the country. The issue affects an estimated 6,700 adults and children in a population of one million. This, according to Hertfordshire county council, is because the area once had three long-stay hospitals which closed some years ago; also because people with learning difficulties are drawn to the locality as some local support networks already exist.

It was three years ago that the People First group, helped by the council, began holding regular meetings with the police and social services in the East Herts area. The police had not realised that the harassment was so widespread. Workshops followed, with both police and the council, and culminated in the launch of an anti-bullying campaign.

The multi-agency approach, entitled People in Partnership, involved Mencap, local advocacy group Pohwer and schools. The seminars, talks at local schools and a resource pack have been so popular that People in Partnership will be launched countywide across Hertfordshire this summer.

The self-help resource pack is crucial to the scheme and is designed to give people advice on what to do when they suffer verbal abuse. Made up of simple words and pictures, and also available on tape, it explains how to report incidents, gives advice on self-protection, information on how to set up local self-help groups and describes what support services are on offer. The resource pack has been updated for the countywide launch. Additions include a reporting form – so incidents can be easily noted by users as they happen – and a wallet-sized card to store vital details such as home and emergency contact numbers and local police information.

The campaign is backed by Mencap – a report published by the organisation three years ago revealed that nine out of 10 people with learning difficulties have been bullied, and many face harassment on a regular basis.

The results of the Mencap report were echoed in a recent straw poll of 106 people with learning difficulties in Welwyn Garden City which showed that 85 of them were bullied while waiting for buses – and the abuse was perpetrated by both adults and children. Other incidents of verbal and even physical abuse occurred in shops, cafes, on public transport or in sports centres.

Many of these incidents are re-enacted in an educational video produced by Mencap, which features several People First members. As well as a learning tool for people with learning disabilities, it is hoped the film will be used in schools to help highlight the issue.

> *A recent poll of 106 people with learning difficulties showed that 85 of them were bullied while waiting for buses*

The campaign has two key messages – try to ignore the bullying and tell someone as soon as you can. As Cooke says, 'You shouldn't bottle it up.'

People First members Derek Weedon and David James, who also works for advocacy organisation Pohwer, feel that the talks at local schools have helped raise awareness. For many members of the group, it was the first time they had interacted

with children without being subjected to verbal abuse by them.

For John Jordan, the campaign has been empowering. 'Children would shout things and throw stones. Now they might still shout out nasty things, but I try and ignore it,' he says. Malcolm Smith, a keen cyclist, used to cut short his cycle trips when he would have to ride past teenage bullies. Now he is learning to disregard their taunts and hopes the teasing will become less frequent as they see it has little effect on him.

The campaign has led another People First member, Richard Blake, to create his own self-help group which should be launched in the next few weeks.

The project is a model of how local authorities, police forces and advocacy groups elsewhere in the country could work together on learning difficulties – something

which affects 1.5m people in England. Indeed, the self-advocacy approach is encouraged by the white paper on learning disabilities, *Valuing People*, which promotes community care, improved day services, social inclusion and a greater say for people with learning disabilities.

'The project started as a real local grassroots piece of work, people with learning difficulties were involved from the outset,' says Cathy Kerr, assistant director of adult care services in Hertfordshire. 'The white paper says that the users should be central – and that's what we've done – it was a project that grew from local initiative.'

For the police, it was, and still is, a learning experience. Hertfordshire chief inspector Nigel Brown says that police have backed up the work with awareness training – teaching officers how to recognise

when someone has a learning problem rather than assuming that person is just being awkward or evasive.

'Historically we've not been that good at meeting the needs of people with learning difficulties in an appropriate way, especially on an operational level on the streets,' says Brown. 'We needed to identify that people need a slightly different approach without being patronising – in terms of interviewing them, facilities for taking statements, advocacy, and so on.

'The bullying of people with learning difficulties is a hate crime – people are being picked on because they're vulnerable – and it has to stop'.

■ This article first appeared in *The Guardian*, 3 April, 2002.

© Saba Salman

A streetwise guide to coping with bullying

Bullying: how can you tell?

Bullying can be obvious – someone hitting you or threatening you – but it can also be harder to pin down. Bullies will often claim that what they are doing is a joke or a game. If in doubt ask yourself:

1. If it is a joke, is everyone laughing?
2. If it is a game, is everyone enjoying it?
3. If it was an accident, is anyone trying to help?

Having fun at someone else's expense is bullying.

Why do people bully?

Bullies are not special, not strong, not tough. In fact they usually need to appear powerful because they secretly feel weak. They may be: jealous of other people; unhappy with themselves; insecure; bullied at home; afraid of being unpopular; unable to show their feelings. They may also be adults. Bullies often try to make it seem that the bullying is the victim's own fault. This is never true.

You are in the middle of a group of people, all laughing at your clothes or hair style. You start off by laughing too but you feel more and more miserable and embarrassed. You try to tell them it's not funny any more but they go on laughing.

Are you being bullied or is this just a joke?
You are being bullied. This laughter is at you, not with you. Do not feel you have to go along with it.

Who is bullying you – everyone in the group? The person who started it? The person laughing loudest?
It may feel as if everyone is bullying you but most people in the group are just following the ring-leader. Do

---

Bullies often try to make it seem that the bullying is the victim's own fault. This is never true.

---

not play the bully's game by concentrating on him or her. Try to pick the weakest member of the group, look them in the face and ask why they are going along with it.

What can you do to stop it – walk away? Hit the ringleader? Yell 'shut up'? Go on laughing?
Do not hit out – you are outnumbered and may be blamed for starting a fight. You are not amused, so why laugh? You can try yelling, but you must make it a loud, angry yell and then walk away at once. Try just walking away.

You try to walk away, they block your path and start pushing you. What do you do?
Be careful how you defend yourself – you do not want to make things worse. You will need to judge the situation: sometimes you can wait these things out, trying to attract attention meanwhile. The best bet might well be to shout loudly, then get away as soon as you can.

Do you tell anyone?

Yes – always tell someone. Go to a sympathetic teacher, explain what happened and identify the bullies. Teachers are now trained to tackle bullying. Tell your friends too – and if they were involved, ask them separately why they did it.

School is out . . .

Bullying sometimes happens on the way to and from school. If this is happening to you, tell a teacher. Their interest in you does not stop at the school gate and they may be able to help. Tell a police officer too – the police are always keen to stop bullying, wherever it happens.

Let them go

If you are bullied for possessions like money, personal stereos, clothes, food or computer games, do not try to hold on to them at all costs. Give them up rather than put yourself in danger, get away as soon as you can. Tell an adult at once. Report it to the police.

Face to face

Bullies often work in groups. Sometimes people who have been friendly to you before will turn on you when they are in a group. Try to find them alone (but in a public place) and ask them each, face to face, why they need to gang up on you. You might prefer to ring them up and talk to them by phone. You might be able to shame them into stopping.

Ways of coping with bullying

1. Ignore nasty comments, insults or teasing. Do not be drawn into arguing.
2. Try not to show you are upset. Do not think of yourself as a victim – you deserve better than that. You have a right to put a stop to this.
3. Tell a sympathetic adult, parent, teacher, relative or friend. Ask them to help.
4. There is safety in numbers. Stay with your friends, or if that is not possible, with groups of people.
5. Shout 'NO' and mean it. Practise in front of a mirror.
6. Walk tall and confidently, even if you feel scared.
7. Do not fight to keep possessions. Your safety is more important.

8. Find out about self-defence classes in your area. These teach you how to respond to different situations and give you confidence.
9. Think before you fight back. You may be making things worse.
10. Get away as soon as you can.
11. If anyone tries to make you feel bad about your race, sex or appearance or abilities do not listen. They are just showing how ignorant they are.
12. It is good to be an individual. If you are different in some way be proud of it.

Things to notice

Do you know someone who is suffering because of bullying? If you have a friend, brother or sister who:
- hates going to certain places
- is unhappy or feels ill at the same time every week
- keeps losing their money or possessions
- has mysterious cuts and bruises
- has become quiet and nervous
- cries at night or in secret

Then this person might well be being bullied. Ask them sympathetically what is wrong and tell an adult you trust about your worries.

Could you be going along with bullying? Could you even be leading it, perhaps without realising? Stop and think – do not make someone else's life a misery.

If you are being bullied, always tell someone. You can do it quietly picking your moment. By telling someone, you can help yourself and possibly help stop other people being bullied.

The Metropolitan Police Service gratefully acknowledges Kidscape for providing many of the suggestions contained on this page. With thanks also to Celestine Keise, General Inspector Islington Education Inspectorate, for her help and advice.

■ The above information is from the Metropolitan Police Authority's web site which can be found at www.met.police.uk

© The Metropolitan Police Authority

Experiences of being bullied

Bullying is widespread. The bullied often admit to bullying others.

Boy bullies' experience of being bullied

	%
Pressurised to join a gang	13%
Bullied outside school	31%
Picked on by a group	49%
Witnessed racism	82%
Experienced racism	15%
Called names	93%
Threatened with violence	58%
Physically attacked in school	51%
Bullying is affecting their life	24%

Girl bullies' experience of being bullied

	%
Victimised by a group	49%
Deliberately left out	66%
Experienced racism	13%
Called names	87%
Blackmailed	25%
Threatened with violence	37%
Pushed or punched at school	48%
Physically attacked	26%

Source: Bullying in Britain – Testimonies from Teenagers, YoungVoice

Schools not addressing bullying problem

By Polly Curtis

Many schools are failing to tackle the problem of bullying, according to research presented at a major conference today.

Despite years of schools attempting to take a tougher line on the problem, two out of three secondary school pupils would still feel uncomfortable telling a teacher they were being bullied, researchers told the ChildLine conference today.

Half of primary school pupils and a quarter of those at secondaries said they had been bullied this term, and more than half from both age groups said bullying was a problem in their schools.

While six out of 10 thought their schools were doing something about it, almost the same proportion said they wanted to be involved in developing anti-bullying initiatives. Schools that did not involve their pupils had higher levels of bullying.

Christine Oliver, from the Institute of Education's Thomas Coram research unit, surveyed 953 pupils in 12 primary and secondary schools for the ChildLine research. She found that although more than 60% of students said their school was 'good' or 'very good' at dealing with bullying, children had very mixed feelings about the benefits of 'telling'.

Ms Oliver explained: 'Teachers and parents rely on pupils to tell them about bullying, but most pupils feel that telling adults is risky because it could make matters worse. Schools need to take action to ensure that the benefits of telling outweigh the risks.

'Effective anti-bullying strategies need to start with adults listening and learning from pupils about their experiences of bullying, how they cope with it, and what their support needs are.'

And she warned: 'It is not enough for schools to parachute in with the occasional anti-bullying initiative. Pupils want schools to tackle bullying over the long term, and most older pupils want to be involved in deciding what to do about bullying in their schools.'

ChildLine is urging schools to give children a say in developing the anti-bullying policies they must have by law, and make more use of children's friendships through peer support and 'buddying' programmes.

> *Half of primary school pupils and a quarter of those at secondaries said they had been bullied this term, and more than half from both age groups said bullying was a problem in their schools*

Its chairwoman, Esther Rantzen, said: 'The message that children are giving through this research can be heard loud and clear – many schools are simply not doing enough to tackle a problem that can be addressed.'

The minister for young people and adult skills, Ivan Lewis, has promised that young people's voices would be heard and their opinions would form a key part of future anti-bullying work undertaken by schools.

ChildLine's recommendations echoed those made in a separate report produced by education watchdog Ofsted. Its report said schools that had the most success in dealing with bullying were ones that 'took full account of pupils' views'.

The Ofsted report, based on visits to six local education authorities in England, said it was good practice to set up safe play areas and quiet rooms, and for staff to supervise children closely at the start and finish of the school day. Like ChildLine, inspectors urged headteachers to make more use of 'positive peer pressure'.

Ofsted chief inspector David Bell said: 'Bullying is a blight that picks off its victims at random, destroying their confidence and making their lives a misery.

'Today's reports from Ofsted and ChildLine are useful tools that teachers and education professionals can draw on as they tackle this unacceptable and insidious behaviour.'

However, Doug McAvoy, general secretary of the National Union of Teachers, said it was difficult for schools to act without the cooperation of pupils and parents. 'Often the bullying takes place away from school premises and out of sight of school teachers. Unless the pupil lets teachers know their hands are tied,' he said.

'Schools try to get this information but they need cooperation from pupils and parents. Sometimes the attitude of parents is to just cope with it or tell their child to bully back. If parents know they should let the school know, if other pupils know they should let the school know. There is a great fear of telling tales, bullying is completely unacceptable but schools cannot act without knowing,' he said.

Ofsted said it was impossible to say whether bullying was on the increase, when greater publicity meant more evidence was coming to light.

Last year, more than 20,000 children contacted ChildLine about the problem of bullying. The subject has been the most common among callers for the last six years.

Giving children a say

By Sally Ferguson

Bullies are making life unbearable for thousands of children across Scotland every day, writes Sally Ferguson. One in four calls to ChildLine Scotland concerns bullying and the issue is so prevalent that the charity has developed a helpline dedicated to taking calls solely on this subject. It has been widely used by children of all ages and backgrounds.

In Scotland, we receive around 6,000 calls a year about bullying. No one deserves to be bullied and our counsellors are there to listen to children and help them decide what to do about it. The old school of thought, that bullying was just a part of everyday life, is slowly being replaced.

Local government has realised the importance of dealing with such issues. Cases such as that of Natalie King, or the recent interdict taken out at Blairgowrie High, bring the issue to the fore. On a positive note, these moves may, hopefully, give schools lax in this area the impetus to get anti-bullying schemes off the ground.

ChildLine's concern, however, is that it can take a long time for cases to go through the courts, thus dragging out what is already an awkward issue. It can also be distressing for children to be in the witness box.

Worried parents can seek advice from many voluntary organisations such as ParentLine Scotland. We advise them to keep the children involved and try not to take over.

> *One in four calls to ChildLine Scotland concerns bullying and the issue is so prevalent that the charity has developed a helpline dedicated to taking calls solely on this subject*

Children can call our helpline and also be encouraged to talk to people around them or seek help from their peers in school youth councils. Young people are subjected to all kinds of humiliation – physical violence, verbal abuse, name-calling – and they often feel they have nowhere to turn.

'I was hit and had my lunch money taken by boys at my school,' said one 14-year-old caller. 'I told my headteacher and my mum. Both said to ignore it.'

One school which tackled the issue is Stonelaw High, Rutherglen. In 2001, an HMI report claimed the school had 'very good procedures'. But some pupils were fearful of being called 'grasses' and a peer mediation scheme was introduced.

The school worked closely with ChildLine and David Mc-Taggart, the assistant head teacher, said the project was a huge success; 95 per cent of pupils thought peer mediation a good idea. The key to anti-bullying policy is involving schoolchildren in the process. Giving them the chance to have a say on an issue which has a big effect on their school life gives them confidence to trust adults and teachers to help them.

■ Sally Ferguson works for ChildLine Scotland. ChildLine's UK-wide 24-hour free helpline is 0800 1111. ChildLine Scotland's bullying line can be reached on 0800 441111, 3.30pm-9.30pm, Monday to Friday. This article first appeared in *The Scotsman*.

© *ChildLine Scotland*

Wise up! to bullying

Young people's rights to do with being bullied

Bullying can mean anything from name-calling and threatening phone calls to being beaten up, constantly left out or ignored. It can happen to anyone, young or old, and anywhere. Is it happening to you or someone you know? Or are you bullying someone?

Did you know . . .

Bullying means constantly treating someone else badly. Even though bullying is painful and damaging, it isn't always taken seriously. But it always should be! It's a form of abuse. It can mean:

- Violence – pushing, kicking or hitting someone
- Words – negative comments, threats, teasing, spreading rumours
- Actions – making fun of someone, deliberately leaving them out of something or being unfriendly, picking on how they look or behave, stealing their things or money
- Racism – jokes, comments, gestures or graffiti about someone's skin colour or culture
- Sexual harassment – making someone uncomfortable by unwanted physical contact or comments about their body, sex or sexuality.

 **Save the Children**

Know your rights

Everyone has human rights. But young people under 18 also have their own set of rights, called the United Nations Convention on the Rights of the Child (UNCRC). Young people are also protected under the UK Human Rights Act 1998.

It's everyone's responsibility to respect your rights. That also means you've got a responsibility to respect other people's rights

---

The UNCRC says you have the right to be protected from any form of discrimination, and from being abused and neglected. You also have the right to be listened to and have a say in decisions that affect you. Adults making decisions about you should always consider what's best for you.

By signing the UNCRC the UK Government has agreed to respect all of these rights and more. The UN makes regular checks to make sure it sticks to its promises.

It's everyone's responsibility to respect your rights. That also means you've got a responsibility to respect other people's rights. For instance, a bystander to bullying has a responsibility to either say something to the people who are doing the bullying, or talk to an adult they trust about it.

Bullying at school

Bullying can happen at school, or on the way to or from school. It can be very hard to talk to someone about it, especially if you feel ashamed, or worried that no one will take it seriously. Remember: being bullied is not your fault!

Try keeping a written record of what's happening – it can be a powerful way to show others what you're going through. If you know an adult who'll listen, try talking to them, or call one of the helplines listed in this article.

All schools must have an anti-bullying policy, but some still don't do enough to stop it. The head-teacher has a legal duty to care for pupils and take action to stop bullying from taking place, so you or your parents could write to him or her about the problem. Maybe you have ideas about how to stop the bullying? Whatever happens, don't resign yourself to being a victim!

You have the right to have your say and be listened to.

Bullying at work

Young people who have part- or full-time jobs may experience bullying at work. It's very common – a third of people who quit their jobs do it because of bullying. Workplace bullying often involves insulting or humiliating someone and attacking the way they act or do their job. Workplace bullies often behave unpredictably and unfairly and abuse their power or position. If you feel unfairly treated or discriminated against at work, you don't have to take it.

You have the right to be protected from discrimination.

Do you bully people?

Just like anyone can be bullied, anyone can bully others. If what you say makes people upset or uncomfortable, you could be bullying them. Think about the pain that it can cause – do you really mean to hurt or upset other people? Do you realise when, why and how you're doing it?

It's important that people who bully others talk to a friend or an adult about their feelings.

Sorting it out

The most important thing you can do about bullying is talk to someone you trust and ask for help. You can also get confidential help and advice from any of the following organisations:

For help with anything, anytime, call ChildLine on 0800 1111 (0800 44 1111 in Scotland) text phone 0800 400 222, write to Freepost 1111, London N1 0BR (no stamp needed), or visit www.childline.org.uk

Freephone the NSPCC's National Child Protection 24-hour helpline on 0808 800 5000 or visit www.nspcc.org.uk

Get Connected, is a free, confidential helpline for all young people (especially if they've run away from home or are thinking about it). Call 0808 808 4994 or visit www.getconnected.org.uk

Bullying Online has lots of advice for pupils and parents who need help with sorting school bullies out. Visit www.bullying.co.uk or e-mail help@bullying.co.uk

Visit www.antibullying.net or call the Anti-Bullying Network on 0131 651 6100 or e-mail abn@education.ed.ac.uk

For advice on dealing with bullying visit www.kidscape.org.uk or call 020 7730 3300.

The Anti-Bullying campaign has trained counsellors giving confidential advice on 020 7378 1446.

For help with bullying at school, visit www.scre.ac.uk/bully

The Children's Society offers under-17s support, advice and information about any particular problem or concern, including abuse. E-mail a Youth Worker on youth-link-advice@the-childrens-society.org.uk, call 0121 236 0323 or visit www.the-childrens-society.org.uk/youthlink

The Andrea Adams Trust gives support, advice and counselling about bullying at work on 01273 704 900. Visit their web site at www.andreaadamstrust.org or email them at mail@andreaadamstrust.org

For lots of information about workplace bullying visit www.successunlimited.co.uk

www.thesite.org/info/careers has step-by-step advice for how to beat bullying at work.

www.dontsufferinsilence.com has information, case studies and links for teachers, pupils and families dealing with bullying.

■ The above information is from Save the Children's web site which can be found at www.savethechildren.org.uk

To order hard copies of the *Wise Up* booklet on bullying, e-mail orders@plymbridge.co.uk or call 01752 202301. The booklets are available in packs of 20 priced at £5.

© Save the Children

Don't suffer in silence

Information about what to do

If you are being bullied
■ try to stay calm and look as confident as you can
■ be firm and clear – look them in the eye and tell them to stop
■ get away from the situation as quickly as possible and
■ tell an adult what has happened straight away

After you have been bullied
■ tell a teacher or another adult in your school
■ tell your family
■ if you are scared to tell a teacher or an adult on your own, ask a friend to go with you
■ keep on speaking until someone listens and does something to stop the bullying
■ if your school has a peer support service, use it
■ don't blame yourself for what has happened

When you are talking to an adult about bullying be clear about:
■ what has happened to you
■ how often it has happened
■ who was involved
■ who saw what was happening
■ where it happened
■ what you have done about it already

If you experience bullying by mobile phone text messages or e-mail when necessary, encourage your parents to report incidents to the police
■ tell a parent, friend or teacher
■ be careful who you give your mobile phone number or e-mail address to
■ make a note of exactly when a threatening message was sent

If you find it difficult to talk to anyone at school or at home, ring ChildLine freephone 0800 1111, or write: Freepost 1111, London N1 0BR. The phone call or letter is free, this is a confidential helpline

■ The above information is from the Department for Education and Skills' web site which can be found at www.dfes.gov.uk

© Crown copyright

Classroom 'courts'

Bullies to be judged by their victims and classmates in school 'courts'

School bullies will be judged by their victims in classroom 'courts' which can tell pupils to pay compensation or attend anger management courses under a scheme being tested across Britain.

Schools in eight counties are to bring in 'restorative justice' schemes in which bullies will be taught the consequences of their actions by facing up to their victims.

The so-called 'bullying courts', chaired by trained mediators, will bring together the perpetrator, the victim, classmates, parents and teachers to decide on an appropriate punishment. Bullies who refuse to accept the court's decision and go along with a 'restorative' punishment can be suspended or expelled.

> *Schools in eight counties are to bring in 'restorative justice' schemes in which bullies will be taught the consequences of their actions by facing up to their victims*

The scheme has received £250,000 from the Youth Justice Board and similar projects are also being paid for by the Government's Children's Fund in an attempt to cut the numbers of suspensions and exclusions from bullying. It has been extended nationwide after a trial in one London borough found that it could cut the numbers kept out of school by up to 70 per cent.

Remedy, a restorative justice and mediation charity, will run the scheme in 20 schools in Barnsley, South Yorkshire. Steve Jones, the project manager, said: 'The person who is causing the harm, the victim and other people who may be affected have their say and come up with a

By Julie Henry

solution. It may be as simple as an apology, or it may be that anger management is the solution – some children admit to problems dealing with their tempers. It is also a forum where parents who are struggling to cope with their children can say so and get some help from parents' support groups or learn about parenting skills.'

The scheme is voluntary and Mr Jones admitted that it would only work if the bully is willing to participate. Schools can insist, however, that if the decision of the conference is not accepted, suspension or expulsion could follow.

'It is not a "court" in that sense because everyone has to agree with the conclusion,' said Mr Jones, 'but it is not a soft option – the punishments they suggest can be quite harsh.'

Schemes run by Youth Justice Teams, an organisation which works with young offenders and is funded by the Home Office, will also be put in place in secondary schools in Oxfordshire, Medway, North Lincolnshire, Somerset, Blackpool, Rhondda and Barnet. The sanctions available to the schools range from an apology to a written promise not to repeat the offence, to lessons in good behaviour.

The technique of restorative justice has been operating in the prison system for more than 10 years and forces criminals to come face to face with the people they have assaulted or robbed. Lord Warner, the chairman of the Youth Justice Board, said that introducing it in schools helped solve immediate problems of bullying but also boosted victims' faith in the justice system.

'It is proving an effective and practical way of nipping bad behaviour in the bud,' he said. 'It shows

a pretty good return rate for kids who otherwise were heading straight out of the school door. I am not saying that there is a 100 per cent success rate but the evidence from this is that the victim is happier than when you don't have some kind of restorative process.'

> *'It is not a "court" in that sense because everyone has to agree with the conclusion but it is not a soft option'*

Youth Offending Teams in the London boroughs of Hammersmith and Fulham and Lambeth have held 132 restorative justice conferences in local schools in the past year. Pupils accused of bullying have signed contracts agreeing to a certain course of action: in up to 70 per cent of cases, this prevented any need for the bully to be suspended.

Veronique Gerber, the headteacher at Hurlingham and Chelsea School, said: 'The project is one of the most successful yet in our school. We have used conferencing for everything from fisticuffs in a science lesson to gang fighting between our pupils and a neighbouring school. Statistics show that students involved in the conferencing do not tend to re-offend.'

Janet Clark, a member of the Youth Justice Team who chairs the conferences at the school, said that bullies were often simply made to give back extorted money or replace broken glasses: in one case, however, the ringleader of a bullying gang agreed to act as 'bodyguard' to a pupil who was being picked on. In another dispute, the solution was for the pupils involved to travel home together on the bus for a week.

Ms Clark said: 'The young people agree to take part because they want to get it sorted. If they are excluded, they still have to come back in to school and the problem is still there. Taking part in conferences seems to reduce the pressure from other pupils who egg them on to fight or bully.'

■ This article first appeared in *The Daily Telegraph*, 18 May 2003.

© *Julie Henry*

You can beat bullying

A guide for young people

Introduction

Nearly everyone is bullied at some time in their lives: by brothers and sisters, by neighbours, by adults or by fellow pupils. If you are being bullied, you may feel scared and vulnerable and quite alone but you owe it to yourself to try and sort out the situation so that the bullying stops. Remember, no one deserves to be a victim of bullying.

It is surprising that all sorts of people who are now very successful adults were bullied when they were young. It is encouraging to know that it is possible to succeed in spite of being tormented at school. All of these well-known people were bullied at school: Kate Winslet, Gareth (from *Pop Idol*), Patsy Palmer (ex *EastEnders*), Victoria Beckham (Posh Spice), Tom Cruise, Sarah Cox and many others.

For some, the bullying went on for years; for others it was less frequent. All of them feel that bullying is wrong and that it was not their fault, but the fault of the bully who was looking for a victim. If you ever bully people, then think seriously about trying to change

> *It is surprising that all sorts of people who are now very successful adults were bullied when they were young*

your behaviour. Nobody really likes bullies. They may be able to frighten people into being nice to them but usually they are unpopular and quite lonely. If you break the bullying habit, you will find it much easier to find good friends.

What can I do if I am being bullied?

Your school may already have a way of dealing with bullying. For example, some schools:

■ have anti-bullying guidelines and procedures for dealing with incidents

■ encourage anyone who is being bullied or who witnesses bullying to tell about it

■ have 'bully boxes' where students put in a note about what is happening

■ have student meetings, circle time or 'courts' where problems like bullying are discussed and dealt with

■ have specially trained students to help each other or teachers who are assigned to help

If your school has an anti-bullying system, use it to get help. If you're not sure how it works, talk to your teacher or Year Head. If your school ignores bullying, don't become resigned to being a victim. You can still help yourself and you can ask others to help you.

■ tell a friend what is happening. Ask him/her to help you. It will be harder for the bully to pick on

you if you have a friend with you for support.

- try to ignore the bullying or say 'No' really firmly, then turn and walk away. Don't worry if people think you're running away. Remember, it is very hard for the bully to go on bullying someone who won't stand still to listen.

- try not to show that you are upset or angry. Bullies love to get a reaction – it's 'fun'. If you can keep calm and hide your emotions, they might get bored and leave you alone. As one teenager said, 'They can't bully you if you don't care'.

- don't fight back, if you can help it. Most bullies are stronger or bigger than their victims. If you fight back, you could make the situation worse, get hurt or be blamed for starting the trouble.

- it's not worth getting hurt to keep possessions or money. If you feel threatened, give the bullies what they want. Property can be replaced – you can't.

- think up funny or clever replies in advance. Make a joke of it. Replies don't have to be wonderfully brilliant or clever but it helps to have an answer ready. Practise saying them in the mirror at home. Using prepared replies works best if the bully is not too threatening and just needs to be

> *'I was always bullied about my glasses. By the time I was 13 I was desperate. Then Mum helped me think up some replies. It felt stupid saying them out loud at home and I didn't think it'd work. The first time I tried one of them out, Paul – the bully – was so surprised, he backed off. Everyone else laughed.'*
>
> Phil, 14

put off. The bully might decide you are too clever to pick on.

- try and avoid being alone in the places where you know the bully is likely to pick on you. This might mean changing your route to school, or avoiding parts of the playground, or only using the common room or lavatories when other people are there. It's not fair that you have to do this but it might put the bully off.

- stick with a group, even if they are not your friends. Bullies tend to pick on people when they are on their own.

- sometimes asking bullies to repeat

If you can keep calm and hide your emotions, they might get bored and leave you alone

---

whatever they've said can take the wind out of their sails. Often bullies are not brave enough to repeat the remark exactly so they tone it down. If they repeat it, you will have made the bully do something they hadn't planned on and this gives you some control of the situation.

- practise 'walking tall' in a mirror. Bullies tend to pick on people they think are weak or timid and they often think shy, quiet people make easy targets. If you look positive and confident, the bully will find it harder to identify you as a target. Pretend even if you only feel two inches high inside.

- keep a diary about what is happening. Write down details of the incidents and your feelings. When you do decide to tell someone, a written record of the bullying makes it easier to prove what has been going on.

- tell your parents or other adults – you need their help. Don't suffer in silence.

■ The above information is an extract from *You can beat bullying – A guide for young people* which is produced by Kidscape. Copies of this publication, in colour and with graphics, can be ordered from Kidscape. See page 41 for their address details.

© Kidscape

Getting help

The young people who have spoken out in this study gave us many clues as to how we can rid our schools of the living hell many children experience. Preventing bullying, however, probably starts long before school entry. There is room for improvement in the number of schools that have effective policies. But when all these fail, young people need someone to talk to. For the bullied this may just make the difference between surviving the torment or never escaping it.

Emotional support – where would you go?			
	Severely bullied	Less severely	Not bullied
If extremely upset, would you phone a helpline? – 'yes'	31.0%	27.8%	19.8%
If you wouldn't phone a helpline why?			
People will think I'm useless	10.0%	4.6%	2.8%
They can't do anything about my life	26.7%	29.7%	21.5%
Would you prefer to use an e-mail helpline instead of a telephone helpline? – 'yes'	30.2%	19.9%	19.8%

The bullies

The tragedy for the bullies is that they do not yet realise that they too need help.

	Have bullied	Never bullied
If extremely upset, would you phone a helpline? – 'yes'	24.8%	25.0%
If you wouldn't phone a helpline why?		
People will think I'm useless	4.5%	4.6%
I don't really understand how they work	7.1%	10.7%
They can't do anything about my life	26.7%	29.7%
Boys don't do this	14.3%	9.7%
Would you prefer to use an e-mail helpline instead of a telephone helpline? – 'yes'	19.9%	22.2%

Source: Bullying in Britain – Testimonies from Teenagers, YoungVoice

Dealing with bullying

Information from KidsHealth.org

You and your friend have walked to school together for as long as you can remember. Lately, though, your friend doesn't laugh and joke like he used to and he seems distracted and jumpy. The other day he actually swore to you he was going to start carrying a weapon.

Maybe your friend is being bullied at school. It happens more than many people may think – about one out of ten teens is the victim of bullying at some point during childhood or adolescence. Maybe in comparison to school shootings like the one at Columbine High School, being bullied doesn't seem all that important. But if you've ever been bullied, you know that's not the truth. Bullying can change everything for you. Read on to learn more about dealing with bullies.

What is bullying, anyway?

Bullying is difficult to define because it can involve so many things. Any subject or person is fair game for someone who bullies. Maybe you've just got braces. At first, your friends teased you a little bit; you figured that would happen. There's one guy at school, though, who takes the teasing to a different level. His tone is mean and hurtful and it's all he ever mentions when you're around. Taunting or teasing like that is a form of bullying.

It doesn't have to be braces; a bully might target anything about you that is different. Maybe you're the tallest girl in your class or you're from an Orthodox Jewish home. Maybe you're Asian or you like to write poetry. And bullying can be done in countless ways: teasing, taunting, ethnic slurs, and sexual harassment are all forms of bullying. What they share is the power to upset or hurt the people who are being targeted.

Bullying can be physical, too. Maybe each time this guy sees you in the hall he intentionally walks into you and then blames you for being in

By Steve Dowshen, MD, and Jennifer Shroff Pendley, PhD

his way. Or you might accidentally knock your books off your desk, only to have him accuse you of trying to trip him. What's even worse is that the bully isn't always just one person; sometimes a whole group singles you out and tries to taunt or hurt you. It can be really scary.

Why are some teens bullies?

Bullies can be tough to categorise. A bully may be outgoing and aggressive, the kind of person who gets her way through force or obvious teasing. On the other hand, a bully can appear pretty reserved on the surface, but may try to manipulate people in more subtle, deceptive ways, like anonymously starting a damaging rumour about someone just to see what happens.

Many bullies, though, share some common characteristics. They are generally focused on themselves and finding ways to seek pleasure. They are often insecure and therefore they may put other people down to make themselves feel more interesting or powerful. For them, it

may be particularly difficult to see things from someone else's point of view. And some bullies act the way they do because they've been hurt by bullies in the past or because another person in their lives – like a parent or other family member – is abusing them in some way.

Standing up for yourself – or a friend

Keep in mind that if you are concerned that you might be in physical danger, you must speak to an adult who can help you. No one wants to rat on someone, but your safety has to be your first priority.

Another thing to remember if you or a friend is being bullied is to avoid being alone. Try to remain part of a group by walking home at the same time as other teens or by always sticking close to friends or classmates, especially before and after school.

If you're being bullied and you're ready to stand up for yourself, there are some techniques you can try:
- Walk away and ignore the bully. It may seem like a coward's response, but it's not. Bullies thrive on the reaction they get and if you walk away, the message is that you just don't care. Sooner

or later the bully will probably get bored with trying to bother you.

- Be confident; walk tall and hold your head high. Use your body language to show that you're not vulnerable.
- Try humour. If you can learn to laugh at yourself then you won't give the bully the response he or she is looking for.
- However you choose to deal with a bully, don't use physical force (like kicking, hitting, or pushing). You can never be sure what the bully will do and violence never solves a problem, anyway.
- Talk about it. It may help to talk to a guidance counsellor, teacher, or friend – anyone who can give you the support you need. Talking can be a good outlet for the fears and frustrations that can build when you're being bullied.

Resisting the temptation to be a bully

It's common for teens to have to deal with a lot of difficult situations and emotions. If you're feeling stressed, angry, depressed, or frustrated, bullying someone else can be a quick escape – it takes the attention away from you and your problems. And if your friends respond by laughing and egging you on, it gives your self-esteem a little boost and reinforces your bullying behaviour. Try to stop yourself right there and think about

how your words and actions can hurt someone else. What may seem like innocent teasing to you can make a huge impact on another person's life.

If you find it hard to resist the temptation to be a bully, you might want to find someone to talk with. Talking can be a good way to release your feelings and frustrations and to look at a situation from a totally different perspective. For example, maybe hearing about how your older brother was bullied when he was in school would cause you to think a bit differently about the way you treat someone.

Getting help

If your school has an antiviolence programme, you might want to

become involved in it. If not, maybe you'd like to start one.

Finally, if your friend is being bullied, see if you can get him to talk to you about it. Then, maybe you can help your friend boost his self-confidence so he can react in a healthy, nonviolent way to the bullying. Try taking a stand by refusing to put up with bullies if you see them in action. If you hear someone taunting a classmate, for example, speak up and point out that this is no way to treat another person. You might be saving someone a lot of pain.

Have you successfully stood up to a bully – or helped a friend stand up to one? Have you put a stop to your own bullying ways? If so, we want to hear from you! Share your tip with other teens by writing to us at teens@kidshealth.org.

Note: All information on TeensHealth is for educational purposes only. For specific medical advice, diagnoses, and treatment, consult your doctor.

- This information was provided by KidsHealth, one of the largest resources online for medically reviewed health information written for parents, kids and teens. For more articles like this one, visit www.KidsHealth.org or else www.TeensHealth.org

© KidsHealth.org

Tackling bullying

**How young people can help schools tackle bullying.
Information from the Anti-Bullying Network**

Who is responsible?

Teachers and parents have a special responsibility for looking after young people and that includes helping them if they are being bullied at school. But adults cannot do this without help from young people. When someone is bullied at school, other young people who are not directly involved usually know what is going on. Even though they are not involved they could help people

who are being bullied. They could encourage them to talk to an adult or could offer to talk to an adult on their behalf. They might be able to let bullies know that they do not like what they are doing and that they are determined to see it stop.

All members of a school community, young and old, have a responsibility to help people who are being bullied and to speak out against bullying behaviour.

Why should young people like you help?

There are many good reasons why young people should help their schools to tackle bullying:

- They might want to help a friend, or someone else they know, who is being bullied.
- Some have been bullied themselves in the past and want to stop it happening to other people.
- They may realise that anyone can

be bullied – if bullying is not challenged it may be their turn to be victims next.

- Taking part in anti-bullying activities can be enjoyable and worthwhile.
- People who watch bullying but do nothing (they are called bystanders) help the bullies by providing them with an audience. Who wants to be accused of helping bullies?

Being cruel isn't cool (a slogan devised in Keith Grammar School).

What if it isn't taken seriously?

If your school is one of those where bullying is still not taken seriously there are things that young people can do to help raise awareness of the problem. Anyone can do this. You just need to be determined to make things change.

Some school students have helped by carrying out questionnaire surveys which can help to show where bullying is happening and how many people are involved. Others have found out about different anti-bullying strategies by reading books and sending away for information. It is best if you can do this as part of the normal activities of the school. Subjects like English, Modern Studies, Religious Studies and PSE (Personal and Social Education) may provide opportunities for work like this. Once your report is ready you could show it to the headteacher, the student council or the school board. This should help everybody to understand that bullying needs to be taken seriously, and that something can be done about it.

How can you help your school?

Many schools are now taking bullying seriously. Here is a list of some of the ways in which teachers and pupils in Scottish schools are dealing with bullying:

- Bully boxes have been set up in some schools. Young people can put notes in these if they are too worried to speak openly about bullying. If your school has boxes like these use them sensibly. Always make sure that anything you write about has really happened.

- Be a buddy to a younger pupil. Older pupils can sometimes volunteer to help new pupils coming into their school by getting to know them and by helping them with any problems
- Special campaigns, such as a 'no-bullying day', can help.
- Some schools have student or pupil councils. You can ask the council to discuss bullying, even if you are not a member.

If young people leave it all to adults, the problem will never go away. You can help to make your school a better place for everyone

---

- Counselling is a special way of talking to someone. People who are being bullied, or who are bullying others, can be helped by counselling, but only if the counsellor (usually an adult) has had training.
- Some schools have set up peer counselling schemes where young people volunteer to learn how to help other young people.
- Mediation – some schools have introduced schemes where two people who disagree about something agree that a third person,

who may be either an adult or another young person, helps to find a solution to a problem. This is helpful in many situations, but not in all cases of bullying. A bully may refuse to take part because he or she has no interest in ending the bullying. A victim may feel that a negotiated solution is not fair when it is the other person who is entirely in the wrong.

- Taking part in plays and other drama activities can help people to understand what it feels like to be bullied and to think about what they can do to stop it.
- Peer Support is an idea, developed in Australia, in which older students volunteer to discuss things like bullying, friendship or drugs with groups of younger pupils.

Don't leave it to others

If young people leave it all to adults, the problem will never go away. You can help to make your school a better place for everyone, and learn some useful skills at the same time, by joining in with activities like those listed above.

■ The above information is from the Anti-Bullying Network's web site which can be found at www.antibullying.net

© *Anti-Bullying Network*

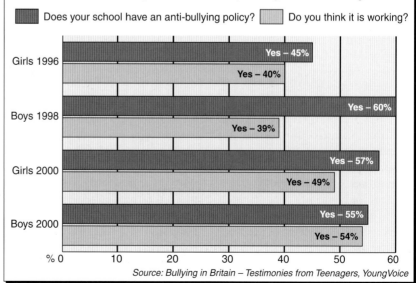

School anti-bullying policies

7,000 young people were asked about anti-bullying policies in their school. 43% of girls and 45% of boys say their school policy still does not have such a policy and of those who said their school did have a policy, no more than 49% of girls and 54% of boys thought it was working.

Does your school have an anti-bullying policy? Do you think it is working?

- Girls 1996: Yes – 45% / Yes – 40%
- Boys 1998: Yes – 60% / Yes – 39%
- Girls 2000: Yes – 57% / Yes – 49%
- Boys 2000: Yes – 55% / Yes – 54%

% 0   10   20   30   40   50   60

Source: Bullying in Britain – Testimonies from Teenagers, YoungVoice

Bullying at work

Quick Facts are a fast, easy way to keep up to date on key people management and development issues and concepts, and offer a starting point for further research. All Quick Facts are available for downloading from the Chartered Institute of Personnel and Development (CIPD) website

This Quick Fact:

- defines bullying and examines its causes and consequences
- provides examples of different forms of bullying
- illustrates the role those with people management and development responsibility can play
- gives elements of an anti-bullying policy.

Becoming aware of the problem

Although it is not new, the problem of bullying in the workplace has only recently become an issue identified by name. Dealing with the effects and causes of bullying is not simple but it is vital for the well-being both of the individual and of the organisation.

In the 1980s, the environment in many organisations became highly competitive, which increased the strain both on managers and on the workforce in general. In 1992, the previously unreported issue of bullying in the workplace received widespread recognition in a BBC radio programme and subsequent book by Andrea Adams[1]. There then followed a series of studies, conferences and research at which the issue was explored, and found to be more widespread than initially realised. It became clear that bullying at work was not a new problem, but that, often for the first time, people were now able to put a name to something that had been causing them misery for many years.

What is bullying?

Bullying is any persistent behaviour, directed against an individual, which is intimidating, offensive or malicious and which undermines the con-

fidence and self-esteem of the recipient. Bullying is largely identified not so much by what has actually been done but rather by the effect that it has on its target.

The Manufacturing, Science and Finance Union (MSF – now Amicus) adopted the following definition of bullying: 'persistent, offensive, abusive, intimidating, malicious or insulting behaviour, abuse of power or unfair penal sanctions, which make the recipient feel upset, threatened, humiliated or vulnerable, which undermines their self-confidence and which may cause them to suffer stress'.

Examples of bullying include:

- verbal or physical threats and intimidation
- persistent negative comments
- humiliating someone in front of others
- unjustified, persistent criticism
- offensive or abusive personal remarks
- setting unattainable targets

- constantly changing work targets in order to cause someone to fail
- reducing someone's effectiveness by withholding information
- ostracism
- picking on one person for criticism when there is a common problem
- not giving credit where it is due
- claiming credit for someone else's work
- belittling someone's opinion
- making false allegations
- monitoring work unnecessarily and intrusively
- undervaluing work done
- removing areas of responsibility without justification
- imposing unfair sanctions.

Bullying by e-mail

Not all bullying occurs face to face. A recently identified problem is that of harassment by e-mail, known as 'flaming'. Prevention of harassment by e-mail should be covered on the overall policies of an organisation.

What bullying is not

Legitimate and constructive and fair criticism of an employee's performance or behaviour at work is not bullying. An occasional raised voice or argument is not bullying.

Strong management or bullying?

Because the perception of bullying is subjective, a management style which, rightly or wrongly, is regarded as normal and is encouraged in one organisation (or even an entire industry) would be totally inappropriate in another situation.

It is unacceptable to condone bullying under the guise of 'strong management'. Conversely, a strong management style is acceptable provided that employees are treated with respect and dignity.

Causes of bullying

In the environment:
Any of the following could be contributory factors.

- Lack of job security.
- Increased pressure on managers to meet targets, often with a reduced workforce.
- An aggressive or authoritarian culture.
- No code of conduct or policy for resolving interpersonal issues.
- Lack of training in management, supervisory and interpersonal skills.

In the person:
There is no easily recognised stereotypical bully (often bullies can be charming to people other than those whom they bully).

Frequently, but not always, the bully is in a position of authority or power, which they abuse by bullying subordinates. There may be bullying at peer group level or even by subordinates or customers.

Anyone can be the victim of bullying, which occurs throughout the organisational hierarchy. Subordinates can bully their bosses, as well as colleagues and peers, and direct reports. People in management or professional positions are most likely to have suffered from workplace bullying – even those in personnel have been the victims of bullying.

Consequences of bullying

For the individual, these can include:

- loss of confidence and self-esteem
- demotivation
- poor work quality and reduced output
- stress-related ill-health
- resignation from work.

For the organisation, these can include:

- increased absenteeism
- increased staff turnover
- industrial unrest
- demoralisation and lack of motivation
- decline in productivity and profit

- decline in staff relations and loss of team spirit
- damage to the organisation's reputation.

The over-riding feature of workplace bullying is that the person being bullied often does not feel that there is anyone to whom they can report the problem. Frequently this is because the bully is their immediate superior so there is no obvious route they can take to report the matter, particularly if the bully appears to enjoy the support of his/her supervisor. In this situation, it is essential that the organisation has in place a policy which will give the victim the confidence to report bullying.

What can an organisation do to help?

- Have a clear code of practice.
- Encourage an open and trusting culture.
- Offer counselling support for all staff.
- Provide suitable management training.

Duty of those with people management and development responsibilities, line managers and witnesses to bullying

The following may improve things, but circumstances vary:

- Be aware of all issues surrounding the recognition and prevention of bullying.
- Ensure that appropriate training programmes are available, particularly in management and supervisory skills and in interpersonal relationships.
- Provide external counsellors (or be trained as counsellors themselves) for employees who are being bullied and who seek support and advice.
- In the absence of trained counsellors, act as an independent arbiter when allegations of bullying are made.
- Carry out employee attitude surveys (particularly if there is a suspicion of bullying), and take action on findings!
- Introduce 360° appraisals.
- Ensure that thorough and well-structured exit interviews are carried out in order to determine whether there is a bullying problem within an organisation.

- If bullying is identified, offer appropriate help to the bully to change the bully's behaviour, or offer them a role with less pressure or opportunity for bullying.
- Return to work interviews.

Elements of an anti-bullying policy

Generally standard grievance procedures are not a suitable means of dealing with bullying. However, there is no need to have a separate bullying policy as it can form part of an existing anti-discrimination or anti-harassment policy. It is important, however, that bullying is clearly identified as a separate, serious issue and not just assumed as being covered by existing guidelines. The policy should:

- make a clear statement, supported by top management, that bullying is a serious offence which will not be tolerated. It could be included as one of the definitions of gross misconduct, for example
- give a definition of bullying which will give employees the confidence to raise the issue and reassure them that their grievance will be dealt with seriously
- explain the procedure to be followed if bullying is alleged
- provide access to counselling and support, either through nominated contact points across the organisation at all levels, or through external contact points, whatever is the most appropriate for the organisation
- guarantee that any complaint will be treated confidentially and will not result in further victimisation
- state the disciplinary measures which will be applicable when bullying is proved.

Reference
1. Adams, A. *Bullying at work: how to confront and overcome it.* London, Virago Press, 1992. ISBN 185381542X

■ The above information is from the Chartered Institute of Personnel and Development's web site which can be found at www.cipd.co.uk Alternatively, see page 41 for their address details.

© Chartered Institute of Personnel and Development (CIPD)

What is bullying?

Information from The Site

Bullying doesn't only happen to school kids, it shows its ugly face in the workplace too.

Harassment, intimidation and aggression are sometimes built into a company's management scheme, or may be carried out by just one individual. Bullying is a gradual process that wears the victim down, and makes them feel worthless, both as a worker and as a person.

What is it?

The Andrea Adams Trust, the national charity against workplace bullying, defines it as:

- Unnecessary, offensive, humiliating behaviour towards an individual or groups of employees.
- Persistent, negative malicious attacks on personal or professional performance, often unpredictable and unfair or irrational.
- An abuse of power or position that can cause anxiety and distress, or physical ill health.

---

*Bullying is
a gradual process
that wears the victim
down, and makes them
feel worthless, both
as a worker and
as a person*

It can take obvious forms, such as physical violence or shouting and swearing, or be subtler, such as ignoring someone, giving them impossible tasks or encouraging malicious gossip about them. Being the best employee in the company is no protection; it may make you the target of a jealous person.

Employees often put up with bullying behaviour because they are afraid of losing their jobs, or think that complaining will make the situation worse.

How to beat bullying

Don't put up with bullying! Here are ten steps you can take to fight it.

1. Deflect the bully if you can. Remain calm, stand firm, and try to keep up a confident appearance. Keep a detailed record of every incident; you will need it as proof if you decide to make a complaint.
2. Check your job description. If you suddenly find yourself being set menial tasks, or are given an increased workload with shorter deadlines, and it isn't in your contract then you can do something about it.
3. Try to get witnesses to bullying incidents, and avoid situations where you are alone with the bully.
4. Get advice from your trade union, or from personnel and health and safety officers at work. Does your employer have a policy on harassment or against unacceptable behaviour?
5. Take a stress management course, and do some assertiveness training. They are good for your general health, and will help you in the future.
6. If you go ahead with a complaint, choose your words carefully. State the facts clearly, but don't get sucked into a slanging match – you could be accused of malicious behaviour.
7. Get emotional support from your family and friends, talk to them about how you are feeling. Ask your GP about counselling. Take sick leave if you need it.
8. If you decide to leave your job because of the bullying, let your company know exactly why you are resigning. It may help others in the future.
9. If you wish to pursue a legal claim against your employer, start by taking advice from your union. If you have a good case, they will take it up on your behalf.
10. Many forms of legal action may be possible, including: industrial tribunals, civil claims for personal injury, and sometimes even criminal action.

The Andrea Adams Trust can be contacted on 01273 704 900.

- The above information is from YouthNet UK's TheSite.org web site which can be found at www.thesite.org

© TheSite.org

Teachers in fear of the bullies

By James Tozer and Sarah Harris

The horrific level of abuse suffered by teachers at the hands of pupils as young as four was exposed yesterday.

A survey of more than 300 schools during a two-week period found almost 1,000 incidents of verbal or physical attacks on staff.

The worst examples included a 15-year-old girl who stabbed a woman teacher three times in the neck with a compass and a nine-year-old boy who threw chairs around and punched and threatened his female teacher.

The survey also revealed a growing trend for girls to take part in abuse – with a quarter of secondary school incidents down to them.

Concerns

The findings reflect concerns about increasing levels of yobbish behaviour among girls.

A recent report found young women were 11 times more likely to be convicted of a crime than 50 years ago.

Last year, Jade Blackburn, 11, was permanently excluded from Wharrier Street Primary School in Newcastle-upon-Tyne for punching deputy headmistress Clare Marriott in the face.

Only a handful of all the incidents reported anonymously to the National Association of Schoolmasters/Union of Women Teachers are likely to ever be recorded officially.

The union says that teachers fear their attackers will go unpunished and that reporting the incidents will merely call into question their own ability to maintain order in the classroom.

Shocked

Staff are also discouraged by the long and complicated forms they have to fill in.

Eamonn O'Kane, general secretary of the NAS/UWT, which conducted the survey in four unnamed local education authorities in the north-west of England, said he had been shocked by its findings.

> 'The depressing reality is that many teachers in our modern schools have to put up with a persistent, high level of abuse'

He called for schools to simplify the process of reporting the abuse of teachers and to clamp down harder on disruptive pupils.

He said: 'The depressing reality is that many teachers in our modern schools have to put up with a persistent, high level of abuse which in any other profession would not be tolerated.'

The union placed incident forms in 304 schools over a two-week period in January. A total of 964 reports of physical or verbal abuse were returned, with attacks by boys and girls of all ages. There were 118 cases of abuse at primary schools, 33 of them involving children swearing at their teachers.

Another 603 were at secondary schools with the rest at special schools. Overall, 126 were physical assaults and the rest verbal abuse. By contrast, two of the authorities taking part in the survey recorded a total of eight cases of verbal or physical abuse officially reported over a whole year. The other two could not provide figures at all.

Tory education spokesman Damian Green said if the union figures were reflected across the country there were likely to be around 200,000 assaults on teachers each year.

A spokesman for the Department of Education said last night: 'Pupils and teachers have a right to learn and work in confidence and safety and anyone who undermines that should be dealt with severely.'

© The Daily Mail, 2003

Bullied at work?

Don't suffer in silence

What is workplace bullying?

Usually, if you genuinely feel you are being singled out for unfair treatment by a boss or colleague, you are probably being bullied. Although there is no comprehensive list of bullying behaviours, and there is no one type of person who is likely to be a bully, the list below should give an idea of some behaviour which constitutes workplace bullying. Bullying behaviour can include:

- competent staff being constantly criticised, having responsibilities removed or being given trivial tasks to do
- shouting at staff
- persistently picking on people in front of others or in private
- blocking promotion
- regularly and deliberately ignoring or excluding individuals from work activities
- setting a person up to fail by overloading them with work or setting impossible deadlines
- consistently attacking a member of staff in terms of their professional or personal standing
- regularly making the same person the butt of jokes

The cost of bullying to you

Stress and ill-health can become part of the daily life of those being bullied. Symptoms can include: anxiety, headaches, nausea, ulcers, sleeplessness, skin rashes, irritable bowel syndrome, high blood pressure, tearfulness, loss of self-confidence, various illnesses of the organs such as the kidneys, thoughts of suicide

The cost of bullying to your boss

Bullying is recognised as a major cause of stress in the workplace and by law, stress must be dealt with in the same way as any other health and safety hazard.

Employers who fail to tackle bullying can pay a high price:

- in lost time – because staff are affected by stress and ill-health

- lost incentive – because morale is low
- reduced work output and quality of service
- and lost resources – because people who are trained, and experienced, leave the organisation
- and if it goes to Employment Tribunal or to court they also face financial penalties and loss of reputation

Most importantly, employers who fail to tackle bullying are breaking the law. That's why it is in everyone's interest to take workplace bullying seriously.

The legal position

Employers have a duty under the Health and Safety at Work Act 1974 to ensure the health, safety and welfare of their employees. If they do not do this they are breaching an individual's contract of employment. It may also be a breach of sexual harassment and racial discrimination legislation as well as the Criminal Justice and Public Order Act 1994. Employers and/or the bully may find themselves facing fines, compensation and possibly a jail sentence.

What to do if you are being bullied

If you feel you are being singled out or bullied at work, you should not have to put up with it. There are steps you can take.

1. First, speak to the bully. A direct approach is usually the best. Tell the person that you find their behaviour unacceptable and ask them to stop. This is sometimes all that is needed. Bullies do not like being confronted particularly by someone who is calm and civilised.
2. The majority of bullying goes on behind closed doors. So tell a friend or work colleague. You may well find out you are not the only one who has suffered. It is important that you do not try to cope on your own.
3. If you are in a union and there is a union safety rep where you work, tell them what has been happening. This will be in confidence and does not mean that a formal complaint will automatically be

made. A safety rep will only do what you want them to and will give you the advice and support you need. They will want to have the bullying stopped quietly and quickly and can go with you to speak to the bully, or see them on your behalf. The safety rep will also help you with a formal complaint, if it goes that far, giving advice and support throughout the procedure.

4. If you are in a union but it is not recognised where you work, call your local union office. The number will be on your membership card or in the local telephone directory. You will still get the legal advice and support you need. Where unions are not recognised, employers are obliged by law to consult the workforce on health and safety issues either directly or through members of staff independently elected as Representatives of Employee Safety (ROES). Where they exist, you should consult the ROES who is likely to be a union member as well.

5. If you are not already in a union – join one. You have every right to do so. You do not have to tell your employers, but if they find out, it is illegal for them to sack you or to cause you detriment. The union will listen to you and ensure you have the best advice. The union can give you free legal

advice, support you, put you in touch with support groups and approach the employer on your behalf.

6. Keep a diary. This will give a vital record of the nature of the bullying and when it occurred. It will be important when the bully is confronted. Many of the incidents may appear trivial in isolation so it is important to establish a pattern over a period of time.

7. Tell your manager or supervisor. If it is one of them who is bullying you, go and tell their manager. Take your diary with you to back up what you have to say. They may not believe you but you have at least told them there is a bullying problem. The more people that know, the more difficult it is for the bully to flourish.

8. In the end you may have to make a formal complaint and go through the grievance procedure.

If you do take this route, never go to a meeting connected with the complaint without your union rep or a friend as a witness.

Get a better deal at work – join a union

When things go wrong at work – be it injury, illness, sex discrimination or bullying – unions are often the only way to secure redress or compensation. Last year alone, union legal services won a record £330 million for their members.

Unions work to ensure the workplace is a healthy environment and tackle sex, race and age discrimination aiming to win opportunities for all. Everyone has the right to join a union and your employer doesn't even need to know you have joined. And at an average weekly rate of only £1.86, joining a union costs less than you think.

To find out more about how to join a union and which is the right one for you, phone the TUC, Britain's national centre for trade unions, on 020 7636 4030 or write to us with your job title, name of employer and the type of industry you work in at: TUC Join a union campaign, Congress House, Great Russell Street, London, WC1B 3LS.

■ The above information is from the TUC's web site which can be found at www.tuc.org.uk

© Trade Union Congress (TUC)

Bullies get to be boss

And they never take the blame. By Darren Behar, Industry Correspondent

Bosses who fly into a rage and blame others when things go wrong are more likely to succeed. Or at least, that's what their staff believe.

Workers questioned for a study said that bullies who rant and rave at every failure have the best chance of promotion, even if they are to blame for the mistakes.

Senior managers are more likely to see such outbursts as a sign of strength than an indicator of poor management skills.

In contrast, it was felt that those who are honest and accept responsibility for errors are likely to damage their prospects.

Workers questioned for a study said that bullies who rant and rave at every failure have the best chance of promotion

---

The problem with all this is that while aggressive bosses are thought to be one of the biggest causes of staff health problems and of reduced productivity, for the aggressor himself such behaviour is seen to pay dividends.

The survey involved 240 students and 120 workers in high-tech companies.

They were presented with a scenario where two executives at an advertising agency were equally responsible for the loss of a client.

One became furious and blamed his colleague, the other accepted part of the blame.

The respondents were asked which was most likely to get promoted. Of the students, 72 per cent picked the angry manager. Nearly two-thirds of the workers agreed.

'In order to succeed in a company that measures people by results, it is not enough just to be good,' said researcher Noga Prat, from the Faculty of Industry Engineering and

---

Workers questioned for a study said that bullies who rant and rave at every failure have the best chance of promotion

---

Management at the Technion Institute in Israel.

'In the event of failure, if you take responsibility, there is a chance that you will be identified with this failure.

If you get angry, you can throw the blame on others and justify yourself.'

However Professor Cary Cooper, an expert in psychology in the workplace at the University of Manchester Institute of Science and Technology, held out some hope for he downtrodden.

The professor said: 'These managers make a lot of enemies, and ultimately those enemies find a way of getting back at them.'

© The Daily Mail January, 2003

Work bullying linked back to school

But company environment is still important

A study has linked bullying at school to bullying in the workplace.

A survey by Professor Cary Cooper and Dr Helge Hoel, at UMIST, and Professor Peter Smith and Dr Monika Singer, at Goldsmiths University of London, found that just over ten per cent of workers reported being bullied in the previous six months. The highest risk of workplace victimisation was for those who had been both bullies and victims at school, supporting suggestions from previous research that this category of schoolchildren should be a focus of concern.

Professor Cooper said: 'We are not saying that all victims at school become workplace victims. But this survey shows how it is essential to work with kids who are bullied or who bully others, so that they can cope with any work problems that may arise later in life.'

The survey of 5,288 adults from workplaces across Britain, *Victimisation in the school and the workplace: Are there any links?* asked respondents to cast their minds back to their schooldays and remember if they were a bully, a victim, bully/victim, bystander or not involved at all.

It also asked which of ten coping strategies they had used when bullied including making fun of it, fighting

Victimisation in the school and workplace

Numbers of respondents bullied in the workplace, and percentages, by primary role recollected at school

Role at school	Proportion bullied at workplace in last 6 months	Proportion bullied at workplace in last 5 years
Neutral	100 8.6%	235 20.1%
Bystander	123 9.7%	253 20.0%
Bully	14 8.6%	41 25.2%
Victim	191 11.2%	482 28.3%
Bully/Victim	118 13.4%	271 30.8%

Source: Professor Cary L. Cooper, UMIST

back, getting help and staying away from school.

Only six per cent reported getting help from teachers. Males more often said they tried to avoid the situation, fought back or tried to make fun of it. Females more often reported that they tried to ignore it, got help or did not really cope.

Respondents who said they did not really cope or used some 'other' strategy when bullied at school were more likely to have been bullied in the previous six months of their working life. The authors suggest that those who did not cope or used some other strategy than those listed were probably not able to use effective

strategies through lack of confidence, lack of social support or other factors with a component of individual psychological characteristics.

Dr Hoel said: 'I must add that many victims of school bullying are not victimised at work and that this suggests the importance of the work environment. Organisational factors in the workplace have an extremely important role in whether someone is bullied or not, so employers bear some responsibility here.'

■ The above information is from UMIST's web site which can be found at www.umist.ac.uk

© UMIST

Bullying rife in Britain's 'caring' jobs

Widespread abuse of employees in NHS is leading to nervous breakdowns and symptoms of post-traumatic stress

By Ben Summerskill, Society Editor

Bullying in the workplace has long been a blight on the business world and an embarrassment to uniformed services, including the police and the Army. But new research confirms it has become just as prevalent in the 'caring' professions.

A nationwide study of staff in the NHS, in healthcare and personnel management, has found that three in five people have witnessed bullying at work in the past two years. One in 10 sufferers show symptoms similar to those of post-traumatic stress disorder. Almost 19 million working days are lost each year in Britain because of bullying at work, say researchers.

'It is disturbing to find such widespread abuse identified among people whose jobs are caring for others,' said psychologist Noreen Tehrani, who carried out the survey. 'In organisations where people are forced to do more and more, bullying appears to become more prevalent.

'Employees don't just feel threatened by physical attacks or hiding things. People can be ignored by colleagues, or have credit taken for their work, or be missed out from social events, or never thanked. When it happens constantly it undermines someone completely.'

> *A nationwide study of staff in the NHS, in healthcare and personnel management, has found that three in five people have witnessed bullying at work in the past two years*

Lyn Witheridge, a former personnel officer from West Sussex, said: 'First you're over-monitored and always watched. Then you're set deadlines with workloads that are impossible to meet. Then guidelines are changed without you being told.

'It happened to me and the accumulation of things over three years resulted in me having a nervous breakdown. If you confront it, you're labelled a troublemaker.'

Witheridge won a financial settlement after going to an industrial tribunal. She now runs the Andrea Adams Trust, advising other victims of workplace bullying.

'I was ostracised at the home where I worked,' said Tim Smith, a former nurse from Birmingham. 'People would go to lunch without telling me so I was left alone. My manager did nothing about it. She also encouraged gossip about my private life.

'After a year I could not get up in the morning. I became lethargic. When my doctor asked about work he identified what was wrong. And when I realised that I was being bullied, I could address it and change jobs.'

Non-violent bullying identified by the survey ranged from unfair criticism to public humiliation in front of colleagues. 'We've seen

people who suffer from flashbacks or nightmares,' said Tehrani. 'This isn't just remembering what happened: it's experiencing the same response as when they were bullied.' Jon Richards of Unison, which represents more than 400,000 NHS staff, said: 'People are under more pressure than ever before. One thing that certainly makes the problem worse is that there is very little training to be a manager in the caring professions.

'Too many people just hide bullying and don't tell people. If you're being bullied by your supervisor or manager, you are very unlikely to report the problem to them. Employers need to work out better ways in which staff can complain if they're being picked on.'

'It is disturbing to find such widespread abuse identified among people whose jobs are caring for others'

Four out of five people who had not reported bullying told researchers it was because 'the bully is my boss'.

Women managers are more likely to be bullied than men but among non-management staff men suffer more than women. The survey will be presented to a conference of the British Association for Counselling and Psychotherapy this week.

The potential costs to employers who fail to tackle bullying are rising. Last year trainee policewoman Angela Vento won £258,000 compensation from West Yorkshire police. She said she was victim of a two-year 'character assassination' by her colleagues and superiors.

It is not only fellow staff who suffer from bullying. 'We recently advised an NHS employee,' said Witheridge. 'He broke down in tears and asked me "How do you think I feel as a carer when I abuse someone I'm meant to be caring for because of the pressures on me?"'

■ This article first appeared in *The Observer*, 12 May 2002.

The 'cancer' of workplace bullying

New Mind guide confronts the 'cancer' of workplace bullying

'I used to be known as a confident high-flyer. Since he took over my confidence has been undermined and I feel under stress at work. He picks on me constantly; it seems nothing I ever do is right. I am always depressed both at work and at home now. It really can't go on, but what can I do, I need this job.'

Mind today launches a new booklet, *How to Deal with Bullying at Work*, that explains how and why bullying takes place in the workplace and what can be done about it.

Bullying at work is hard to measure, but is undoubtedly destructive and causes misery to thousands of men and women every working day. Put simply, workplace bullying means someone abusing his or her power or position to undermine an individual's ability or to intimidate someone in a way that makes him or her vulnerable, angry and powerless.

Interestingly, the *targets* of bullying are often seen as more capable, successful and popular than the bully themselves. But it is a need to control others that primarily drives the bully. Most bullies are in positions of authority – managers or supervisors.

Because bullying is rarely confined to open abuse, it can be difficult to recognise and confront, particularly if the individual is being undermined by the behaviour. Mind's new guide offers clear examples of open, hidden and even unconscious bullying to help the reader understand and identify the behaviour in all its forms.

The effects of being bullied can be felt both physically and emotionally and should not be underestimated. It has been likened to a cancer that creeps up on someone long before they are aware of what it is that's making them feel its ill effects.

How to Deal with Bullying at Work explores the choices left open to someone being bullied, from confronting the bully, to seeking help, to taking legal action. For example, often it is safer to seek advice from personnel or union representatives and to follow the company's official grievance procedures than to challenge the individual head-on.

■ *How to Deal with Bullying at Work* is available from Mind Publications, 15-19 Broadway, London E15 4BQ priced £1 plus a 44p A5 SAE. Tel: 020 8221 9666 or email: publications@mind.org.uk alternatively visit their web site at www.mind.org.uk

Army acts as 43% of troops condemn bullying

Over 40% of the British army believe soldiers suffer from bullying, sexual discrimination, and harassment, according to a private poll carried out by the Ministry of Defence.

The poll, released to Paul Keetch, Liberal Democrat defence spokesman, comes at a time when the army is embroiled in a growing controversy over the deaths of four soldiers in the Deepcut barracks in Surrey.

As many as 43% of soldiers responding to questions in the ministry's internal survey said they believed the army had a problem with harassment, discrimination, and bullying. The survey was conducted by QinetiQ, the ministry's research agency.

More than 5% said they had personally experienced bullying, and 11% believed it was a problem in their own unit. A further 4.7% complained of sexual discrimination or harassment, and 3.8% of racial discrimination or harassment.

'The survey will make uncomfortable reading for the government and will spark alarm with the families of armed forces personnel,' Mr Keetch said yesterday.

By Richard Norton-Taylor

'Army personnel, those best able to judge the situation for themselves, see bullying as a serious problem.

'Forces families have every right to expect a robust protection system in place for young recruits facing the scourge of bullying'.

> *As many as 43% of soldiers said they believed the army had a problem with harassment, discrimination, and bullying*

'At a time when our armed forces are struggling to recruit and retain, the perception that bullying is rife will do little to attract people to the ranks,' Mr Keetch said.

The figures were disclosed by Adam Ingram, the armed forces minister, after persistent pressure from the Liberal Democrats on the MoD to release the results of the army's 'continuous attitude survey'.

The survey was carried out in March and April this year and sent to a 4% random sample of trained soldiers, excluding Gurkhas and reservists. Of the 3,978 questionnaires which were sent out, 2,037 were returned.

An army spokeswoman said yesterday that the 43% figure reflected perception rather than reality. She added that the MoD was working on moves, including awareness of equal opportunities, to back up its policy of zero tolerance towards bullying and discrimination.

'It is certainly not something we turn a blind eye to. Cases are fully investigated and can result in dismissal,' she said.

Mr Ingram last month announced an 'appraisal' of the army's training procedures. The move was prompted by the deaths at the Royal Logistics Corps barracks at Deepcut. The army has told families of the victims that it believes the cause was suicide.

The campaign for a public inquiry into treatment of soldiers at Deepcut gathered momentum last month when 116 MPs signed a motion urging government action, and the families expressed anger at the way their children's deaths had been investigated.

The families believe that there is evidence of a culture of bullying that might partly explain why there have been 1,800 non-natural deaths in the army over the past 12 years, including 188 shootings.

Concern about treatment of squaddies at Deepcut has grown since the family of Private Geoff Gray questioned the army's claim that their 17-year-old son had shot himself before a proper investigation had been started.

In March, a coroner delivered an open verdict on Pte Gray, saying: 'I do not find that he took his own life.'

Workplace bullying

Information from the Suzy Lamplugh Trust

Workplace bullying means unwanted, offensive, humiliating, undermining behaviour towards an individual or group of employees. This abuse of power or position can cause such chronic stress and anxiety that people can suffer physical ill-health and mental distress as a result.'

(Diana Lamplugh OBE)

No one should have to endure being bullied at work but the Suzy Lamplugh Trust recognises that standing up to bullies is rarely simple. If someone is being bullied, it is important that they talk about their situation with someone they trust, e.g. a partner, friend or doctor, before they make any decision as to what action to take. If they do decide to 'take on' the bully, they must understand that their situation may well become more unpleasant before it improves – if it ever does.

The Suzy Lamplugh Trust has a network of Training Consultants throughout the UK. Their experience of dealing with bullying in the workplace is that simple solutions, such as moving individuals to different positions within organisations, are not the answer. Bullying is often part of the culture of a company or organisation and, if this is the case, radical change is needed. At the very least, it is necessary to look at the circumstances that led to the bullying and change them.

No one should have to endure being bullied at work but the Suzy Lamplugh Trust recognises that standing up to bullies is rarely simple

---

Some victims of bullying do feel strongly enough about their rights, and angry enough about the treatment they have received, to want to expose the bully and put a stop to their behaviour. These people should be given as much help and support as possible. Everyone they work with will owe them a debt of gratitude, as bullying in the workplace will continue as long as the bullies are allowed to get away with it.

However, some people do not want to go through the stress of taking on the bully, especially when they feel there is little chance of a successful outcome. In cases where there is a 'culture of bullying', complainants may even have reason to believe that they will end up taking on their entire organisation. People in this position should consider leaving their jobs. This is not a negative course of action – on the contrary, these people have made a positive decision that will enable them to gain control. Everyone should remember that their personal safety, health and well-being are more important than anything else.

■ The above information is from the Suzy Lamplugh Trust, visit their web site at www.suzylamplugh.org Alternatively see page 41 for their address details.

© The Suzy Lamplugh Trust

Bullying and harassment at work

Guidance for employees

Everyone should be treated with dignity and respect at work. Bullying and harassment of any kind are in no one's interest and should not be tolerated in the workplace, but if you are being bullied or harassed it can be difficult to know what to do about it. This article:

- gives employees[1] basic information about bullying and harassment
- summarises the responsibilities of employers
- outlines some of the options open to you
- points you to sources of further information and advice.[2]

What are bullying and harassment?

These terms are used interchangeably by most people, and many definitions include bullying as a form of harassment. Harassment, in general terms, is:

- unwanted conduct affecting the dignity of men and women in the workplace. It may be related to age, sex, race, disability, religion, nationality or any personal characteristic of the individual, and may be persistent or an isolated incident. The key is that the actions or comments are viewed as demeaning and unacceptable to the recipient.

> *Bullying or harassment may be by an individual against an individual or involve groups of people*

Harassment can also have a specific meaning under certain laws (for instance if harassment is related to sex, race or disability, it may be unlawful discrimination). By December 2003 there will also be protection against discrimination on the grounds of religion or belief and sexual orientation.

Bullying may be characterised as:

- offensive, intimidating, malicious or insulting behaviour, an abuse or misuse of power through means intended to undermine, humiliate, denigrate or injure the recipient.

Bullying or harassment may be by an individual against an individual (perhaps by someone in a position of authority such as a manager or supervisor) or involve groups of people. It may be obvious or it may be insidious. Whatever form it takes, it is unwarranted and unwelcome to the individual.

Examples of bullying/harassing behaviour include:

- spreading malicious rumours, or insulting someone by word or behaviour (particularly on the grounds of race, sex, disability, sexual orientation and religion or belief)
- copying memos that are critical about someone to others who do not need to know
- ridiculing or demeaning someone – picking on them or setting them up to fail
- exclusion or victimisation
- unfair treatment
- overbearing supervision or other misuse of power or position
- unwelcome sexual advances – touching, standing too close, the display of offensive materials
- making threats or comments about job security without foundation
- deliberately undermining a competent worker by overloading and constant criticism
- preventing individuals progressing by intentionally blocking promotion or training opportunities.

Bullying and harassment are not necessarily face to face. They may also occur in written communications, electronic (e)mail, phone, and automatic supervision methods such as computer recording of downtime from work or the number of calls handled if these are not applied to all workers.

Bullying and harassment make someone feel anxious and humiliated. Feelings of anger and frustration at being unable to cope may be triggered. Some people may try to retaliate in some way. Others may become frightened and demotivated. Stress, loss of self-confidence and self-esteem caused by harassment or bullying can lead to job insecurity, illness, absence from work, and even resignation. Almost always job performance is affected and relations in the workplace suffer.

Responsibilities of employers

Employers are responsible for preventing bullying and harassing behaviour. It is in their interests to make it clear to everyone that such behaviour will not be tolerated – the costs to the business may include poor employee relations, low morale, inefficiency and potentially the loss of staff. An organisational statement to all staff about the standards of behaviour expected can make it easier for all individuals to be fully aware of their responsibilities to others.

Under the Health and Safety at Work Act 1974 your employer has a legal responsibility to ensure that your health, safety and welfare at work are protected. There is a right to mutual trust and confidence between employer and employee; and if bullying or harassing behaviour are allowed to go unchecked, that could mean that such trust and confidence is lost. Employers are usually liable in law for the acts of their workers, and this includes bullying or harassing behaviour.

The Sex Discrimination Act 1975, the Race Relations Act 1976 and the Disability Discrimination Act 1995 make unlawful any bullying or harassment that includes elements of discrimination, for instance sexual harassment or gender-related bullying behaviour.

By December 2003 there will also be protection against discrimination on the grounds of religion or belief and sexual orientation and by December 2006 on the grounds of age, following the implementation of the EU Employment and Race Directives.

The Government intends that employees will receive a specific and free-standing right to be protected from harassment in all five areas – race, sex, disability, religion or belief and sexual orientation – and will introduce a standard definition of harassment (with a modified definition for sexual harassment). For the latest information visit the Employment Relations section of the Department of Trade and Industry website at www.dti.gov.uk/er

Certain types of harassment, such as stalking, are covered in criminal law by the Protection from Harassment Act 1997, and the Criminal Justice and Public Order Act 1994.

The Employment Rights Act 1996 gives protection to employees with qualifying service by allowing them to claim 'unfair constructive dismissal' if they are forced to leave their job because of the actions of their employer. Such actions might include failure by the employer to deal with any complaint of bullying or harassment, or failure to protect their employees from bullying and harassing behaviour.

What can you do?

Bullying and harassment are often clear cut but sometimes people are unsure whether or not the way they are being treated is acceptable. If this applies to you there are a number of things to consider, including:

- has there been a change of management or organisational style to which you just need time to adjust – perhaps because you have a new manager or work requirements?
- is there an organisational statement of standards of behaviour that you can consult?
- can you talk over your worries with your personnel manager, your line manager/supervisor, union representative or colleagues, who you may find share your concerns?
- can you agree changes to workload or ways of working that will make it easier for you to cope?

If you are sure you are being bullied or harassed, then there are a number of options to consider, and these are set out below. You should take any action you decide upon as quickly as possible.

Let your union or staff representative know of the problem, or seek advice elsewhere, perhaps from a Citizens' Advice Bureau, an Acas enquiry point or one of the bullying helplines that are now available by phone and on the Internet.

Try to talk to colleagues to find out if anyone else is suffering, or if anyone has witnessed what has happened to you – avoid being alone with the bully.

If you are reluctant to make a complaint, go to see someone with whom you feel comfortable to discuss the problem. This may be your manager, or someone in personnel (particularly if there is someone who specifically deals with equality issues), your trade union representative, or a counsellor if your organisation has suitably trained people available.

Keep a diary of all incidents – records of dates, times, any witnesses, your feelings, etc. Keep copies of anything that is relevant, for instance annual reports, letters, memos, notes of any meetings that relate to your ability to do your job. Bullying and harassment often reveal themselves through patterns of behaviour and frequency of incidents. Keep records and inform your employer of any medical help you seek.

Tell the person to stop whatever it is they are doing that is causing you distress, otherwise they may be unaware of the effect of their actions. If you find it difficult to tell the person yourself, you may wish to get someone else – a colleague, trade union official or confidential counsellor – to act on your behalf.

If you cannot confront the bully, consider writing a memo to them to make it clear what it is you object to in their behaviour. Keep copies of this and any reply.

Be firm, not aggressive. Be positive and calm. Stick to the facts. Describe what happened.

If you do decide to make a formal complaint, follow your employer's procedures, which should give you information about whom to complain to and how your complaint will be dealt with.

If you have access to a union representative or other adviser, ask them to help you state your grievance clearly, as this can help in its resolution and reduce the stress of the process. Most employers have a grievance procedure which will be used to handle your complaint, and some organisations have special procedures for dealing with bullying or harassment. After investigating your complaint, your employer may decide to offer counselling or take disciplinary action against the bully/

If you cannot confront the bully, consider writing a memo to them to make it clear what it is you object to in their behaviour

harasser in accordance with the organisation's disciplinary procedure.

Disciplinary procedures may also be used for disciplinary action against someone who makes an unfounded allegation of bullying or harassment.

What about taking legal action?

If despite all your efforts, nothing is done to prevent the mistreatment, you should take advice on your legal rights. If you leave and make a claim to an employment tribunal, the tribunal will expect you to have tried to resolve the problem with the organisation, and any records you have kept will be considered when it hears your claim. This is also the case in claims alleging discrimination, where you might still be employed by the organisation. Resignation may be the last resort but make sure you have tried all other ways to resolve the situation.

Where can you get help?

Additional advice can be obtained through the Acas National Helpline. Advice can also be obtained from your trade union, legal advisers, Citizens' Advice Bureaux and in relevant cases, the Commission for Racial Equality, the Equal Opportunities Commission and the Disability Rights Commission.

There are also bullying helplines available, such as the UK National Workplace Bullying Advice Line (tel 01235 212286), and the Andrea Adams Trust (tel 01273 704900).

Bullying help sites can also be found on the Internet – search under 'Workplace Bullying'.

It can sometimes help to read of other people's experiences and what they did about it. One such book is by Andrea Adams, called *Bullying at Work: How to confront and overcome it* (published by Virago in 1992).

Notes

1   The term 'employees' is used to cover all those who work for someone else rather than on their own account, regardless of whether they are employed strictly under a contract of employment.

2   This information was revised at date of printing – April 2003. Legal information is provided for guidance only and should not be regarded as an authoritative statement of the law which can be given only by the courts. Legal considerations must be looked at in the light of the particular circumstances, and it may be wise to seek legal advice. The Acas National Helpline can provide information on employment matters but cannot provide legal advice on particular cases. Other sources of information and advice for employees include trade union representatives, Citizens Advice Bureaux, and lawyers.

■ The above information is from the Advisory, Conciliation & Arbitration Service's web site which can be found at www.acas.org.uk

© Advisory, Conciliation & Arbitration Service (ACAS)

Spotting the signs

Workplace bullies can pick on anyone: man or woman, black or white. It is that arbitrary. Bullies often get away with it by making victims think it's their fault. Learn to spot the signs and fight back – with GPMU

What is bullying?

Workplace bullying is generally vindictive, cruel, malicious or humiliating behaviour towards an individual or even a group of employees. It is demeaning and can cause untold stress and suffering to those on the receiving end.

There's nothing new in this – what is new is acknowledging that it reaches far beyond the playground, and crops up where you may least expect it. It may occur between workers but equally, it can be the abuse of authority by management. It may reflect a management style that is autocratic and based on telling people what to do rather than allowing them any personal initiative.

Bullies can be motivated by a number of things such as lack of self-confidence, envy towards other people's abilities, success and popularity or they may take a completely irrational dislike to an aspect of someone's personality or their way of doing things.

Workplace danger signs

Evidence shows that bullying is most likely to occur in workplaces where there is/are:

- fear of redundancy
- an extremely competitive environment
- fear for one's position
- a culture of promoting oneself by putting colleagues down
- envy among colleagues
- an authoritarian style of management and supervision
- organisational change and uncertainty
- little participation
- lack of training
- de-skilling
- no respect for others and their point of view
- poor work relationships generally
- no clear codes for acceptable conduct
- excessive workloads and demands on people
- impossible targets or deadlines
- no procedures for resolving problems

Bullying can cause untold stress and suffering

Bullying can take many forms such as: open aggression, threats, shouting, abuse, ridicule, excessive supervision, and constant criticism.

How bullies operate

Bullies may also take the credit for a person's work, never the blame, over-rule a person's authority, remove whole areas of work responsibility from the person, give them only routine tasks which are well below their capabilities, set impossible targets, constantly change a person's duties without telling them and then criticise or discipline the person for not meeting those demands, withhold information, ostracise and marginalise their target, exclude the person from discussions or decisions, spread malicious rumours, refuse requests for training or block a person's promotion.

Bullying may occur in front of other employees who then become too afraid of becoming the next target to do anything to help the person being bullied, but sometimes it can be more subtle and harder to detect. It can often happen where there are no witnesses. The victim is often too afraid to complain and worried that they will not be believed in any case.

■ The above information is from the Graphical Paper Media Union's (GPMU) web site which can be found at www.gpmu.org.uk

© *Graphical Paper Media Union (GPMU)*

KEY FACTS

■ 1 in 4 children in the UK have been bullied or threatened via their mobile phone or PC according to a survey commissioned by leading UK children's charity NCH. (p. 3)

■ Mobile phones appear to be the most commonly abused medium with 16% of young people saying they'd received bullying or threatening text messages, followed by 7% who had been harassed in Internet chat-rooms and 4% via e-mail. (p. 3)

■ In a recent large-scale survey in Britain, more than half the young people questioned had been bullied and one in ten had been severely bullied. A third of the girls and a quarter of the boys had at some time been afraid of going to school because of bullying. (p. 5)

■ Bullying can include all kinds of negative behaviour, both direct and indirect, which is designed to hurt and humiliate. The main defining feature of this behaviour is that it involves a systematic abuse of power – there is a perpetrator who exerts power and control and a victim who is helpless and powerless. (p. 5)

■ In a recent study of 3,000 girls, over half had been bullied and 12 per cent had been severely bullied (Katz et al 2001). It has been suggested that girls are more involved in sustained bullying than boys (Ofsted 2001) and that it is girls who report more fear of attending school because of bullying. (p. 5)

■ In racist bullying, a young person is targeted for representing a group and attacking the individual sends a message to that group. (p. 6)

■ 51 per cent of schools reported at least one incident of homophobic bullying occurring in the last term, but only six per cent of schools had bullying policies that specifically mentioned homophobic bullying. (p. 6)

■ In a recent survey, three-quarters of the young people questioned felt that their school does not have an effective anti-bullying policy that works. (p. 7)

■ Research shows that up to 40% of young lesbian, gay or bisexual people have attempted suicide because of bullying at school. Three-quarters of those being bullied have a history of truancy. (p. 11)

■ A report published by Mencap three years ago revealed that nine out of 10 people with learning difficulties have been bullied, and many face harassment on a regular basis. (p. 12)

■ Bullies often work in groups. Sometimes people who have been friendly to you before will turn on you when they are in a group. (p. 14)

■ Many schools are failing to tackle the problem of bullying, according to research. (p. 15)

■ Despite years of schools attempting to take a tougher line on the problem, two out of three secondary school pupils would still feel uncomfortable telling a teacher they were being bullied. (p. 15)

■ Half of primary school pupils and a quarter of those at secondaries said they had been bullied this term, and more than half from both age groups said bullying was a problem in their schools. (p. 15)

■ One in four calls to ChildLine Scotland concerns bullying. (p. 16)

■ Schools in eight counties are to bring in 'restorative justice' schemes in which bullies will be taught the consequences of their actions by facing up to their victims. (p. 19)

■ Pupils accused of bullying have signed contracts agreeing to a certain course of action: in up to 70 per cent of cases, this prevented any need for the bully to be suspended. (p. 19)

■ Bully boxes have been set up in some schools. Young people can put notes in these if they are too worried to speak openly about bullying. If your school has boxes like these use them sensibly. (p. 24)

■ Some schools have set up peer counselling schemes where young people volunteer to learn how to help other young people. (p. 24)

■ Peer Support is an idea, developed in Australia, in which older students volunteer to discuss things like bullying, friendship or drugs with groups of younger pupils. (p. 24)

The Andrea Adams Trust, the national charity against workplace bullying, defines it as:

■ Unnecessary, offensive, humiliating behaviour towards an individual or groups of employees.

■ Persistent, negative malicious attacks on personal or professional performance, often unpredictable and unfair or irrational.

■ An abuse of power or position that can cause anxiety and distress, or physical ill health. (p. 27)

■ A survey of more than 300 schools during a two-week period found almost 1,000 incidents of verbal or physical attacks on staff. (p. 28)

■ A study has linked bullying at school to bullying in the workplace. (p. 31)

■ A survey found that just over ten per cent of workers reported being bullied in the previous six months. (p. 31)

■ Four out of five people who had not reported bullying told researchers it was because 'the bully is my boss'. (p. 33)

■ Women managers are more likely to be bullied than men but among non-management staff men suffer more than women. (p. 33)

■ Over 40% of the British army believe soldiers suffer from bullying, sexual discrimination, and harassment, according to a private poll carried out by the Ministry of Defence. (p. 34)

ADDITIONAL RESOURCES

You might like to contact the following organisations for further information. Due to the increasing cost of postage, many organisations cannot respond to enquiries unless they receive a stamped, addressed envelope.

Advisory, Conciliation & Arbitration Service (ACAS)
Brandon House
180 Borough High Street
London, SE1 1LW
Tel: 020 7210 3613
Web site: www.acas.org.uk
ACAS publishes a series of reading lists on work-related issues including job sharing, flexible work hours, part-time work and homeworking. National helpline: 0845 7474747.

Anti-Bullying Campaign (ABC)
185 Tower Bridge Road
London, SE1 2UF
Tel: 020 7378 1446
Fax: 020 7378 8374
Telephone advice line open Monday to Friday, 9:30am to 5:30pm.

Chartered Institute of Personnel and Development (CIPD)
CIPD House, Camp Road
Wimbledon
London, SW19 4UX
Tel: 020 8971 9000
Fax: 020 8263 3333
Web site: www.cipd.co.uk
With over 105,000 members, it is the professional body for those involved in the management and development of people.

ChildLine
45 Folgate Street
London, E1 6GL
Tel: 020 7650 3200
Fax: 020 7650 3201
E-mail: reception@childline.org.uk
Web site: www.childline.org.uk
ChildLine is a free, national helpline for children and young people in trouble or danger. Provides confidential phone counselling service for any child with any problem 24 hours a day. Children or young people can phone or write free of charge about problems of any kind to: ChildLine, Freepost 1111, London N1 0BR, Tel: Freephone 0800 1111.

Graphical Paper Media Union (GPMU)
Keys House, 63-67 Bromham Road
Bedford, MK40 2AG
Tel: 01234 351521
Fax: 01234 358558
E-mail: general@gpmu.org.uk
Web site: www.gpmu.org.uk
The world's largest media trade union.

Kidscape
2 Grosvenor Gardens
London, SW1W 0DH
Tel: 020 7730 3300
Fax: 020 7730 7081
E-mail: contact@kidscape.org.uk
Web site: www.kidscape.org.uk
Works to prevent the abuse of children through education programmes involving parents and teachers.

MIND
Granta House, 15-19 Broadway
Stratford, London, E15 4BQ
Tel: 020 8519 2122
Fax: 020 8522 1725
E-mail: contact@mind.org.uk
Web site: www.mind.org.uk
Mind works for a better life for everyone with experience of mental distress.

NCH
85 Highbury Park
London, N5 1UD
Tel: 020 7704 7000
Fax: 020 7226 2537
Help line: 08457 626579
Web site: www.nch.org.uk
NCH works to improve the lives of Britain's most vulnerable children and young people.

Save the Children
17 Grove Lane
Camberwell, London, SE5 8RD
Tel: 020 7703 5400
Fax: 020 7703 2278
E-mail: enquiries@scfuk.org.uk
Web site: www.savethechildren.org.uk
Save the Children is the leading UK charity working to create a better world for children.

Schools Health Education Unit (SHEU)
Renslade House
Bonhay Road
Exeter, EX4 3AY
Tel: 01392 667272
Fax: 01392 667269
E-mail: sheu@sheu.org.uk
Web site: www.sheu.org.uk
Promotes objective debate about the best ways to serve and educate young people and students about health and social issues.

The Suzy Lamplugh Trust
14 East Sheen Avenue
London, SW14 8AS
Tel: 020 8392 1839
Fax: 020 8392 1830
E-mail: trust@suzylamplugh.org
Web site: www.suzylamplugh.org
The Suzy Lamplugh Trust is the national charity for personal safety. It aims to create a safer society and enable people to live safer lives, providing practical personal safety advice for everyone, everyday, everywhere.

Trades Union Congress (TUC)
Congress House
23-28 Great Russell Street
London, WC1B 3LS
Tel: 020 7636 4030
Fax: 020 7636 0632
E-mail: info@tuc.org.uk
Web site: www.tuc.org.uk
The TUC has over 75 member trade unions, representing nearly seven million people from all walks of life.

YWCA
Clarendon House
52 Cornmarket Street
Oxford, OX1 3EJ
Tel: 01865 304200
Fax: 01865 204805
E-mail: info@ywca-gb.org.uk
Web site: www.ywca-gb.org.uk
The YWCA in England and Wales is a force for change for women who are facing discrimination and inequalities of all kinds.

INDEX

ACKNOWLEDGEMENTS

The publisher is grateful for permission to reproduce the following material.

While every care has been taken to trace and acknowledge copyright, the publisher tenders its apology for any accidental infringement or where copyright has proved untraceable. The publisher would be pleased to come to a suitable arrangement in any such case with the rightful owner.

Chapter One: Bullying at School

Half the population are bullied . . . , © Success Unlimited, *On-line bullying*, © NCH, *E-bullying*, © NCH, *Bullying by mobile phone and cell phone*, © Success Unlimited, *If looks could kill*, © YWCA, *Bullying, what to do, what not to do*, © 2003 Pupiline Limited, *Fear of being bullied*, © Schools Health Education Unit (SHEU), *'I sometimes bully people. What can I do?'*, © Kidscape, *Stress of young bullying victims*, © The Daily Mail, April 2003, *Hidden damage*, © Guardian Newspapers Limited 2003, *Bullying tactics*, © Saba Salman, *A streetwise guide to coping with bullying*, © Metropolitan Police Authority, *Experiences of being bullied*, © YoungVoice, *Schools not addressing bullying problem*, © Guardian Newspapers Limited 2003, *Giving children a say*, © ChildLine Scotland, *Wise up! to bullying*, © Save the Children, *Don't suffer in silence*, © Crown copyright is reproduced with the permission of Her Majesty's Stationery Office, *Classroom 'courts'*, © Julie Henry, London 2003, *You can beat bullying*, © Kidscape, *Getting help*, © YoungVoice, *Dealing with bullying*, © KidsHealth.org, *Tackling bullying*, © Anti-Bullying Network, *School anti-bullying policies*, © YoungVoice.

Chapter Two: Workplace Bullying

Bullying at work, © Chartered Institute of Personnel and Development (CIPD), *What is bullying?*, © TheSite.org, *Teachers in fear of the bullies*, © The Daily Mail, 2003, *Bullied at work?*, © Trade Union Congress (TUC), *Bullies get to be boss*, © The Daily Mail, January 2003, *Work bullying linked back to school*, © UMIST, *Victimisation in the school and workplace*, © UMIST, *Bullying rife in Britain's 'caring' jobs*, © Guardian Newspapers Limited 2003, *The 'cancer' of workplace bullying*, © 2003 MIND (National Association for Mental Health), *Army acts as 43% of troops condemn bullying*, © Guardian Newspapers Limited 2003, *Workplace bullying*, © The Suzy Lamplugh Trust, *Bullying and harassment at work*, © Advisory, Conciliation & Arbitration Service (ACAS), *Spotting the signs*, © Graphical Paper Media Union (GPMU).

Photographs and illustrations:

Pages 1, 10, 16, 27, 29, 34, 36, 39: Simon Kneebone; pages 5, 12, 22, 32, 35: Pumpkin House; pages 7, 11, 20, 28, 38: Bev Aisbett.

Craig Donnellan
Cambridge
September, 2003